Born to Be Unstoppable:

My Kenyan Story, Global Journey and Life's Legacy™

Wanjiku Kironyo

Published by Fifty Fifty Limited
PO Box 6807-00200
Nairobi, Kenya.
Email: info@fiftyfiftyltd.com

Book ISBN: 978-9966-097-28-6
Wanjiku Kironyo
E-mail: info@wanjikukironyo.com
Web: www.wanjikukironyo.com

DEDICATION BY WANJIKU KIRONYO

To my parents Julius Mukuria and Damaris Nyambura and my own grandmother Eunice Wanjiku for trusting to send that skinny girl from the small village of Cura out into the world with nothing more than the belief that there is nothing too great for me to accomplish. To my son Kironyo and daughter Wandia, in your eyes I was capable of greatness. Here is to giving me a chance to write about my greatest moments in life and for times that you have watched me rise and fail and still encouraged me to keep going.

TABLE OF CONTENTS

BORN IN UNCERTAIN TIMES

"It is how we embrace the uncertainty in our lives that leads to the great transformation of our souls". – Brandon A

Being born in the 1950s, especially in Colonial Kenya, was considered a tragedy; a sad twist of fate that signified a dire destiny. It was a catastrophe, and a hard nut handed down by the harshness of nature at a most inopportune time.

To be born in the fifties could only mean two things for a black Kenyan; you were either going to die from poverty or from an askari's bullet. Even if you survived either of these two fates, your death sentence could still have come in the form of the dreaded typhoid or a horde of other nasty infections which the missionaries and white doctors never really understood.

I was born in 1952, in Central province. At the time, my parents lived in a small village called Cura, located in Kabete district. This was the year when the British declared a state of emergency in Kenya and sent their mighty military to quell the Mau Mau rebellion, a revolutionary movement that started during the long period of political unrest among the Kikuyu people who were one of the most exploited communities under colonial rule. I was born to Kikuyu parents and to a community that was, and still is the largest ethnic group in Kenya.

My parents named me Wanjiku. Neither my parents nor I had a hand in choosing that name. The names of Kikuyu girls were all predetermined according to their order of birth, following long-standing Kikuyu customs. Being the second female child, I had to be named after my maternal grandmother, Eunice Wanjiku, wife of Maruri. At the time, whether my parents liked it or not, the name Eunice was bestowed upon me. Had I been the first female child, I would have been named after my paternal grandmother, Irene Wanjiru.

"Uncertainty is where things happen. Where the opportunities for success, for happiness, for really living are waiting"

I was later baptized Eunice Esther Wanjiku as having two Christian names was popular during that time. I however preferred the name Esther, which sounded youthful, unlike Eunice, which to me sounded extremely elderly. I remember the village folk would actually pronounce it as "Eunithi" which I really hated. Fortunately, my friends preferred to call me Esther, and the name stuck to my great pleasure.

My mother was quite fond of me, mostly because I was slim and quick to carry out my chores. My constant hard work coupled with cases of malnutrition brought about by lack of a proper diet, led to my slim and slender physique. I was energetic and hardworking, running around and hurrying over all my tasks, and although my mother sent me on almost every errand, she was cautious about letting me handle brittle household items like glass cups and plates. This was because I always did things hastily and was likely to drop and break things quite unceremoniously.

I have four sisters and four brothers. I can still vividly recall the times some of my siblings were born. My mother would appear twice her size and would often complain about aching feet. The older children would then take over all the housework.

Most of the women in our community were skilled in midwifery, and all the pregnant women would be monitored keenly. The women would update each other on any new developments, and they knew exactly when a child was due. There was an experienced traditional midwife and about three or four other women who knew how to assist in delivery. Before giving birth, a woman in the preparation for her own delivery would set aside a brand-new ball of thread and a razor blade, which would be used to tie and cut the umbilical cord.

I remember when my youngest brother, Oscar was born. It was late into the night, and my sisters and I were all fast asleep on the bed that we all shared at the far end of the room. Njeri, our youngest sister at the time, was sandwiched in between us in order to prevent her from falling off the bed.

We were poor and therefore could not afford to have individual beds. My brothers also shared a bed and if you were lucky to be the only boy or girl child in your family, you would sleep by yourself while the other same sex children shared a bed. Our poverty-stricken state meant that each group had to share a single blanket and old pieces of clothes and rags would be used as mattresses.

As the night wore on, we suddenly heard our mother calling out loudly. We quickly got out of our beds and ran to her side. She instructed us to light the kerosene lamp, while she ordered my brother to round up the midwives. Thanks to their constant monitoring and experience in child care, they were already anticipating the birth and had prepared themselves beforehand.

Upon their arrival, we were hurriedly sent back to our beds, but we dared not sleep. My sisters and I sat on our beds, silent and wide-eyed, listening excitedly to everything that was going on while anxiously waiting for the morning, knowing that we had a new person to welcome to the family.

Our house had no ceilings so we could hear everything clearly. They began the process of delivery, and I would hear the ladies asking for various items like water or a razor blade. All this was efficiently carried out in a very professional manner. We listened quietly as my mother screamed and after what seemed like an eternity of excruciating pain, we heard the sound of a baby crying as he took his first breath.

I was very anxious to see the outcome of the process, and so I quietly walked to my mother's room and stood at the door, peering in. Her now grayed out hair looked like a snug-smothered hat, and her eyes had shrunk deep into their sockets. I stood there wondering if she could actually see at all.

When we found out that the baby was a boy, we immediately knew that he would be named Machara, after my mother's brother. Finally, I heard the midwives proclaim joyfully in the Kikuyu tongue, "Machara has arrived! Machara has arrived!"

The next morning, after they had cleaned up the delivery room, we were allowed to go in and see the new baby. I remember how excited we were to find a baby boy whose skin was as light as that of a white baby. Over the next few days, as my mother convalesced, the women of the village cared for my mother and would prepare special meals for her. Sometimes, after she had eaten her fill, or didn't feel like eating much, she would share her meals with us. These were some of the perks that came with a newborn baby.

THE FEARLESSNESS AND AUDACITY OF MY MOTHER

"Successful mothers are not the ones who never struggled. They are the ones who never give up despite the struggle". – Sharon Jaynes

In the early 1900s, Kikuyu society was predominantly patriarchal. Girls were expected to grow up to be homemakers and farm workers, never engaging in 'masculine' tasks such as having a formal job, engaging in business and aspiring to leadership positions in the community. Women were subjected to male dominance and whatever a father or husband ordered was obeyed without question.

When the white settlers came, they brought new technologies and ideas with them. Many Africans adopted the white man's way of life. Fathers began sending their daughters to school and mothers began to work and engage in business. My mother was one of such women. Armed with sheer will and a brilliant mind, she carved for herself a path that was the envy of every woman in the village.

My mother's name is Damaris Nyambura. She came from a polygamous family she is the third born of seven siblings. I was fortunate enough to have known her brother and two sisters as the others had already passed on by the time I was born.

My mother was very close to her siblings and in turn, a close bond developed between us, her children and my aunts and uncle. She was also very close to her father, and he treated her as his favorite child, so much so that he never had a meal without sharing it with her. There was, however, a conflict between my mother and her brother because he received a lot of favoritism from my grandmother. Anything nice from my grandmother went straight to him. For some strange and inexplicable reason, the women would lean towards the male children who were mischievous and would not do much work, while the men favored the female children.

My mother rose to become more than just another victim of this cultural system. She embraced peasantry with unreserved fervor and became the first woman in Cura to rear grade cows for commercial purposes. She was also the first woman to deliver milk on a bicycle, first to learn how to use a sewing machine and first woman to chair the local cooperative. She was indeed a dynamo of energy and pioneer of ideas.

In colonial times, white settlers carved out large tracts of land for themselves and turned them into coffee, tea and pyrethrum farms. The black men and women were expected to labor on these farms but were never given the opportunity to grow their own cash crops or own any of the land. It is this unspoken policy that infuriated many Africans and led them to come together and begin their own cooperative movement. Therefore, they would be economically empowered to farm their own land with their own crops.

I remember one day, waking up in the middle of the night, startled by the sound of a sewing machine. I got out of the bed and tiptoed towards the sound, only to find her tailoring by the flickering light of her smoky tin-lamp.

My mother never let anything go to waste. When a dress in her possession was about to get torn, she would take the dress apart and turn it into a shirt for my brother or alternatively, make dresses for my sisters and I. Our fashionable dressing was solely attributed to my mother. She was also very active among the village women and portrayed very good leadership skills, especially in the women's union. Many times I would also see her teaching the women how to knit as well as many other skills.

"When you live for a strong purpose then hard work isn't an option it is a necessity"

My mother did everything differently and in style. As a result, our neighbors accorded her much respect and were very envious of her abilities. As a little girl, I watched my mother turn our home into a small marketplace. The neighbors constantly trooped in to either get jobs on the farm or have their clothes mended.

As aforementioned, she did not spare us from her firm belief in hard work and discipline. She was a pacesetter and often led by example. When the farm hands came to work, my mother would make us join them so that we could speed up the work. Working alongside the laborers in the farm taught us to be humble and never to regard others as lesser human beings.

On the other hand, we were never fully trained in skills like farming and knitting because my parents did not see those as sustainable sources of income. Their goal was to give us an education so that we wouldn't have to work with our hands like they did. They never encouraged us to work on the farm, but instead used the experience to motivate us to work hard in school so that we could have better lives.

My children were also greatly impacted by my mother. My daughter Wandia recalls her grandmother's story as one of will-power, persistence, and principle. She looks up to her grandmother as a woman who pushed herself beyond her point of endurance so that her children would have hope and a future. A resilient woman who worked day and night on her farm so that she would have enough to provide for her children, enough to share, store and enough to sell. Wandia has many times been inspired by her uncles and aunties. She has seen in them the value of service, sweats and smarts, discipline and delayed gratification and they, in turn, passed these values on to her and her brother Kironyo.

My mother's intellect constantly amazed my children. They both fondly speak about their grandmother as the only Kikuyu grandmother they know who can talk to her grandchildren intelligently about Martin Luther King and Caesar Chavez, revolutionaries who fought for freedom many miles from her East African village.

Today, arthritis has stolen the spring in my mother's step, and age has mellowed the intensity in her eyes. I hope that my life is a tribute to my mother, who taught me how to embrace life and strive to live each day with passion and humility, determined to make a positive difference in the society.

MEMORIES OF MY GRANDMOTHER

"My grandmother made a decision to live her life with kindness and grace. Her strength inspired others to do the same." – Wanjiku Kironyo

Another strong woman who influenced my life greatly was my father's mother, Eunice Wanjiku, who I happened to be named after. She was the last and most loved of my grandfather's four wives. I remember my grandmother as a slim and tall woman, of very few words. Like my mother, she was also very hard-working and had gone through her share of struggles in life which made her quite reserved and guarded.

My grandmother's story is one that began in sadness and misfortune. A few months after marrying my grandfather, my grandmother gave birth to perfectly healthy twin boys. Unfortunately, during that time, superstition was deeply entrenched in African cultural belief systems. Anything that the people did not understand was interpreted as a bad omen, which had to be purged. This was done in order to cleanse the people and the land and ultimately to prevent the judgment of the gods.

Birthing twins was one of such bad omen. For the new mother and child to be accepted by the society, one of the twins had to be murdered.

My grandmother watched in horror as one of her sons was put to death by suffocation. As if that wasn't enough punishment, a few years later her second son developed complications and passed away and years later, she lost yet another child; a beautiful baby girl.

The trauma from the death of her children, coupled with the struggles and oppression during the Mau Mau freedom war and the state of emergency never left my grandmother.

One could clearly see the sadness in her eyes. She chose to cope with her depression by burying herself in her work and was always found toiling in the farm.

She and I became very close from very early on. At one point, my mother began taking classes in animal husbandry at the nearby Waruhiu farm. Whenever she had to leave for her classes, she would leave us in the care of our grandmother, which we loved because unlike our mother, she was very laid back so we knew we could get away with a lot of mischief.

Sometimes my siblings and I would come home very late from playing outside with our friends and instead of scolding us, my grandmother would only warn us not to repeat the offense, and that was the end of that. Afterwards, we would join her in the kitchen, which was a separate room outside the main house. There we would sit around the fire and roast maize and potatoes while narrating stories of what had happened that day to each other.

I personally took great delight in accompanying my grandmother to different places. Sometimes we would visit her relatives, sister or her daughter (my aunt) who resided in the endmost part of the city. She would treat us to sweets and pastries, such as *Samosas*, *Mandazi*, and Soda. When we accompanied her to the market, she would send us to different shops and stalls to get her everything that she needed, which we did with enthusiasm because we knew that there would be many treats afterward.

She valued education and would constantly remind us to stay focused in our pursuit of academic success because to her, it was imperative that we excelled in school in order to become successful in future. She was very candid in her discussions with us and even spoke to us openly about relationships with boys. I fondly recall her sternly warning us girls against allowing men into our lives before we were old enough to start dating.

She would say to us that if we did so, they would chew us up like roasted potatoes and spit us out like sugarcane after they had enjoyed all the sweet juice. Her warnings and tales about how boys would take advantage of unsuspecting naïve girls ensured that we did not engage romantically with boys until we completed our education.

I remember the first time I went in search of a job. I was in high school at the time and was lucky enough to land a job during the holidays at a national museum in Nairobi. In those days, students rarely received any formal employment while still in school.

However, a friend of mine mentioned that the museum was giving students internship positions to keep them busy during the holidays.

Working at the museum exposed me to a whole new world, where people sat behind desks as they worked, as opposed to farming and sewing as people did in the village. The director of the museum was a lady from Uganda who was very humble and well-respected. This was very inspiring for me as it was the first time I had seen a woman in such a highly-regarded leadership position.

My first salary was a cool 150 shillings, which at the time was a lot of money for a student. The first thing I thought of spending my money on was a gift for my grandmother, to show her my deep appreciation for everything she had done for us. I went into town and chose the most beautiful piece of fabric I could find, which my mother later turned into a dress for my dear grandmother. I also gave my other siblings some money to spend on themselves.

Years later, after I completed my O-level education, I left Kenya for the United States in order to further my education. After seven years in America, I was overjoyed to find her alive and well when I returned. Unfortunately, a few months after I arrived she developed dementia and from then, her mind dulled slowly by slowly until she passed on.

INSPIRATION OF A FATHER

"My father gave me the greatest gift anyone could give a person. He believed in me."
– Jim Valvano

I miss my grandmother dearly. She was a kind and gentle soul who wished only the best for her loved ones. She was also a great influence on my father, as he is the embodiment of her laid-back and lenient character. The shrewdness of my character comes from my mother; but the finer qualities of my personality, attitude, and fiber comes from my father.

My father struck anyone who met him as a cool but strong personality, despite his quiet, mostly unvoiced presence. He came across as a man on the inside of a personal inner sanctum—where no sleaze or greed has set foot. At 89, my father lacked the prevalent babbling personality of men his age, who constantly rant about themselves and their youth in conceited nostalgia.

My father, JM Ng'ang'a, was never overbearing in his old age. He had none of the arrogance most men in the society his age would ooze whenever they had an audience. He never tried to impress his visitors and was hardly domineering. Indeed, he was quite the family man and never showed favoritism to either one of his children. He would sometimes refer to my sister Joyce as "his sister" for she was named after his own sister.

My father also had a very good relationship with his mother in law—my maternal grandmother. They had mutual trust and respect for each other. From an early age, they enjoyed a very good relationship. He knew that she expected him to value honesty, be trustworthy, and to impart the value of education to her grandchildren. Sometimes they would even form business partnerships, buying bananas from Githunguri, where he worked, and she would sell them at the market.

My father was the oldest amongst his siblings, and he was admired because of his love for education. He attended Githunguri High School, where he worked hard and spent most of his time concentrating on his studies. The school focused mainly on educating students that had a passion for Kenya's liberation and those with a keen interest in politics—unlike others like Alliance High school which were founded by missionaries and focused on teaching religion.

Teachers at Githunguri High School taught politics and religion from their own perspective and not from what the colonizer wanted the Africans to hear. Students who went to this school, including the first president of Kenya; his Excellency the late Jomo Kenyatta, maintained their African roots and more specifically their African name. This they did so as to reject the brainwashing that took place in Christian schools where students were made to drop their names and use English names. The students in these schools were so ingrained in the white culture that they looked down on their African counterparts, and some going as far as referring to them as primitive.

My father, on the other hand, appreciated the African way of learning where he was given the opportunity to embrace his culture. As a result, he studied hard, taking advantage of every opportunity he could get to learn the African system and beliefs. His studies were however suddenly disrupted by the Second World War as he and many other Africans were dragged into a conflict they neither started nor knew anything about.

While in Burma, my father started out as a wound dresser, caring for soldiers wounded in the war. He then developed an interest in medicine, and when he returned to Nairobi, he attended the King George Medical Institute where he was trained as a clinical officer, specializing as an anesthesiologist.

On completion of this intensive course, my father went on to become one of the first Africans ever to be trained at the Kenyatta National Hospital. He loved to read and always brought large volumes of books home with him. This, coupled with his medical training and experience, made him extremely knowledgeable. He would even teach and train Africans as well as white people on the management and treatment of tropical diseases like Malaria.

As a medical practitioner, my father was well-respected in the community. People would come from far and wide to consult him on health issues. I recall a particular boy who was brought to see my father by his parents. His hair had turned a strange reddish-brown color and I eavesdropped on my father's conversation with the boy's parents. He advised them that their son was suffering from malnutrition, and he needed to eat a balanced diet in order to restore his health.

When I think about this man, my father, I always remember him as a quiet person. However, this was not always the case. I was surprised one day when I went to the hospital where he was working at the time and found him deeply engaged in an animated conversation with several people. I remember thinking to myself, in disbelief, that I had never thought it possible he could speak for so long. In society, he was a very well respected man.

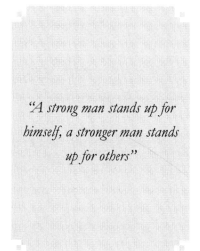

"A strong man stands up for himself, a stronger man stands up for others"

My father was one of the few educated men and there were always very high expectations of him concerning not only his family but also the community. For this reason, he always maintained a silent and reserved demeanor. However, while around his colleagues, he was more relaxed and open to conversation without feeling the pressures of being judged or the responsibilities that came along with his status in the society. By disposition, he observed a lot and said very little.

I could have been doing something very mischievous, and my father would not say a word, but just sit and watch me in my mischief. Instead, he would wait until evening and call me to the sitting room and say something like, remember I saw you climbing the tree? Do you realize how dangerous it is? Why were you climbing the tree? Do you know you could break your legs or worse? As was his nature, the greater emphasis of the questioning revolved around taking precaution. Never would he attack and scold us; instead, he always gave us sound advice.

My mother was the parent we feared. She was a zealous disciplinarian and the one who administered physical punishment on our backsides whenever we erred. My father, on the other hand, would only insist on knowing why you acted recklessly. He never perceived us as girls who would become women condemned to limited, finite roles. He wanted his girls to be everything they imagined they could be and he'd show us that it was possible.

Whenever we went anywhere, my father would point out things and explain them to us so that we may take on the world with confidence and a winning attitude. When it came to finances, he discussed everything with my mother and even encouraged her to invest their money in worthwhile ventures while he was away at the hospital. In turn, my mother didn't let him down as she wisely invested in many ventures, including a portfolio of valuable pieces of land. By choosing to empower his wife, and never suppressing her creativity and ambition as most men of his time did, he played a huge role in creating an independent women out of my mother, my sisters and me.

My father was instrumental in helping me realize that women were just as capable as men and that I could also rise to achieve my wildest dreams. Whenever I visited him at the hospital, he would always introduce me to his female colleagues. I vividly remember one beautiful Jamaican doctor who had very long hair, great skin complexion, and pleasant manner. There was also an Indian lady who was in charge of the X-ray department. The way my dad introduced them to me and even from the way he interacted with them, I got the message that women do rise to high positions in life. The message rang through my mind clearly that a woman could be an achiever.

Since I was a little girl, my greatest source of inspiration has been my own family: My strict and industrious mother who taught us to be hard workers. My soft-spoken but loving grandmother whose sound advice enabled me to weather my teenage years and school life and my dear father who pulled me out of my shell and taught me to reach for the stars. They were the solid foundation on which my story began. I strongly believe that it was his attitude that got our family to where we are today.

A BLOODY WAR

"War does not determine who is right only who is left". – Bustrend Russell

I was born at the height of the Mau Mau resistance. Back then, bloodshed and chaos were the order of the day. Although I cannot recall much of the first three years of my life, I do remember that the days and nights were constantly filled with gunshots and terror.

I saw many dead bodies while living with my parents in the local hospital's compound. Countless bodies of lifeless Mau Mau fighters who had died in battle would arrive in an old, shattered Bedford-stretcher that doubled up as an ambulance. The bodies were dumped in mass graves that had been dug near the staff quarters. As a child, I did not understand much about death as a permanent state, and thus, the sight of hundreds of dead bodies did not affect me as much as it should have.

As the anti-British war raged on, suspicion was heightened, and neighbors distrusted each other because there was no way of telling who genuinely supported the cause and who was a British spy. I vividly recall four men being butchered in our school compound, murdered by the Mau Mau right before our very eyes on suspicion of being British spies.

One of the four men was dragged away from our classroom where he had hidden from his assailants.

From the late '40s and into the early '50s, the British adopted a divide-and-conquer strategy to subdue unity and resistance among Africans. This strategy consisted of splitting entire communities into groups, which were then constantly moved from camp to camp. During that time, my father worked and lived within the hospital compound. Hospital quarters for Africans consisted of a one-roomed house which came with a small kitchenette. If you had a family, you would sub-divide the small room into sections using what was called a 'badhia'. This was basically a large sheet or piece of cloth extended from one side of the room to the other. The name was derived from the Swahili word 'pazia', which means curtain.

Since my father was working in the medical field, he would often be shifted from one district hospital to another whenever the need arose. Some of the places where he worked included Meru, Kiambu, Embu, Muranga, Tigoni, and Isiolo districts. For a while, my siblings and I moved around with our father until a time came when he felt that all the movement was negatively impacting our education. At the time of this decision, he was housed in a facility that unfortunately did not allow him to accommodate his wife and children and as a result, we were forced to separate from my father. He remained at his station, while my mother and we the children moved back to the village.

Even though we were supposed to reside in the village, we still found ourselves moving back and forth between the hospital and the village. This was because of the oppression and insecurity in the camps at the time, many of which were at the hands of British minions, known as "Home Guards." Home Guards were local villagers turned British collaborators and selected as British representatives. The settlers did not enforce the law which they imposed on the Africans themselves. Rather, they used the Home Guards while ensuring that they monitored everything and everyone very closely. The Home Guards were allocated standard issue police whips, which they used ruthlessly on any villager—young or old—who dared to defy them.

Life in the camps was hard. The home Guards would order the villagers to dig deep, wide trenches all around the camps and then lay row after row of barbed wire within the trenches so that it would be impossible for people to leave the villages unless they used the main entrance. This was meant to ensure that they knew where everyone was at all times. If you wanted to leave, you had to get permission from the Home Guards and report back to them when you returned.

There were random roll calls which the adults had to attend. Failure to appear for roll call would earn one a serious beating from the Home Guards. Surprisingly, despite the threat of the menacing whip, many defiant adults would skip roll call, hiding under beds and in the bushes when the Home Guards came looking for them. Since the Home Guards were locals, they quickly noticed when anyone was `missing at the roll calls or in the trenches. They would then go to the absentee person's house and threaten the children into telling them where their parents were. Some children, out of fear, would give away their parents' hiding positions. They would then pull the adults out from under the beds or from nearby bushes and whip them thoroughly as their children watched in terror.

My own mother once tasted the burning lash of a Home Guard's whip and that fateful day is forever burned into my memory. It was about

10 AM in the morning when this fierce-looking man appeared out of nowhere, ready to beat us all senseless. My mother, having known that the man was on his way, had safely tucked herself away under our only bed, in the farthest, darkest corner she could find. We cowered and trembled in fear as the man shouted at us, wanting to know her whereabouts.

The older children were brave enough not to give her away and one by one we all said that she had left for an unknown place. However, when my youngest sibling was questioned, he got so frightened that he told the man where our mother was hiding. With a devilish grin on his hard face, he kicked in the door of our hut, pulled her out and proceeded to hand her the beating of a lifetime. Even today, my mother still bears the crisscrossed scars of the lashing that she received on that day.

THE STATE OF EMERGENCY

"Peace is not the absence of war but the presence of justice"

During the state of emergency, many Africans were arrested and tortured by the British. The tension was very high in those days, and all Kikuyus were suspected of aiding and sympathizing with the Mau Mau. Even those Africans who had previously served the white settlers faithfully as servants became suspects. This was because the Mau Mau had managed to convert some of these domestic workers and laborers into spies and executioners. As a result, no African was trusted and inevitably my father became a victim of British paranoia. He was accused of being a Mau Mau spy, and we were all arrested. My father was whisked away, while my mother and us, the children, were held at a women's camp. The women were placed in solitary confinement, where they were scrutinized and interrogated for hours on end and I recall my mother was tasked with the duty of taking out the buckets of waste and emptying them into the sewer.

The long nights were usually the worst times of our stay at the facility. The air would be filled with blood-curdling screams and cries of women who were being tortured. My siblings and I would begin to sob, but mother would angrily hiss at us to shut up so as not to attract any attention to ourselves. As children in the camp, we lived in constant fear, not aware of why we were being subjected to such persecution.

The village camps consisted of rows of L-shaped houses referred to as Royals, as well as round mud huts that were referred to as 18s. The round huts acquired their name due to their design, which consisted of eight posts distributed in a circle that was 18 feet wide. The 'Royal' was a codename for those villagers who leaned towards the white man's way of life as opposed to observing cultural rites and traditions. Those who lived in the 18s and those living in the Royals were encouraged to rival each other openly despite both groups being subjected to forced labor by the British. This rivalry worked well for the British because it kept the Africans distracted, busy fighting amongst themselves instead of focusing on the real enemy.

As time went on, this rivalry went from bad to worse and in the end, entire communities and families were torn apart by this system. It was common to see a man and wife living on the royal side of the village with his children attending the local school, while his uncles lived across the divide in the 18 huts with their daughters already circumcised and ready to be married off at fourteen.

In the early 1900s, African communities already had thriving medical and political systems in place. Each community had its own remedies and treatments for various illnesses as well as skilled midwives to help in the delivery of children. However, as the British became more hostile towards communities that resisted their dominion, they began introducing deadly pathogens into the environment in order to weaken them.

Even today, the Africans still believe that syphilis was introduced into the Maasai community because they were hostile towards the British. Syphilis was however spread as a result of wife sharing, a common practice in the community. It was normal for people to share their wives amongst their peers. If for example one's husband was involved in organizing a circumcision ceremony with a group of people, they were now entitled to sleep with your wife and it became an honor for men to share their women with other men. This meant diseases were carried and spread easily within the community.

The plague disease, which was unheard of before the settlers appeared, also claimed the lives of many people. This disease wiped out thousands of Kikuyu folk, including one of my grandfather's wives and seven of her 8 children. Traditional medicine men were powerless against these new illnesses, and the British denied the Africans proper healthcare. Countless people died as a result.

As a result of the poor living conditions in the camps, diseases like cholera and dysentery spread like wildfire. I remember a time when one of my brothers almost died of diarrhea. I wasn't spared either. At a very young age, I developed glaucoma, as well as a nasty skin infection which spread all over my body. Death, especially in little children, was very common in the '50s and hardly a week passed by without a death in the village. Such was life, growing up under the iron grip of British rule. Somehow, my family was always able to survive all the hardships we faced. Days turned into weeks, weeks into months, and months into years. It was as if the more oppression we were subjected to, the more resolved we became to overcome. Determined to survive, we soldiered on as the war raged on.

DEALING WITH THE BLEAKNESS OF VILLAGE LIFE

"Hardships often prepare ordinary people for an extraordinary destiny."
– CS Lewis

Growing up in the village, we would hear amazing stories of white people swimming in the ocean and in man-made swimming pools. Although we never got the chance to enjoy the beach or exclusive pools in our younger years, we did have the river. Whenever it rained heavily, and the water levels in the normally shallow river rose, all the children would troop down to the river for a swim.

I vividly remember sneaking out of school one day to go swimming. Of course, I was spotted by my sister, who didn't waste any time reporting my mischief to Mother. Later that afternoon when I got home in my soaked clothes, I tried to sneak into the bedroom without anyone noticing. Little did I know that my now furious mom had been waiting for me to return back home. In one powerful sweep, she flung me onto the table and proceeded to give me a severe beating, all the while telling me how dangerous swimming in the river was.

I didn't take her warnings seriously, and soon reverted back to my old ways. Two years later, a group of children from our village drowned in the deep-water storage reservoirs that were located next to the river. Up to that point, I had been completely unaware that the villagers had dug very deep holes in the bank of the river, which were used to store rainwater as well as that from the overflowing river whenever it flooded. After a heavy rainfall, one could not tell where these reservoirs were located, and unfortunately, the children accidentally fell in and drowned. Needless to say, I became more careful after that.

Because of the boyish tendencies, I had when I was younger, I often engaged in all sorts of risky activities like climbing to the top of tall trees and swinging from their branches. We would also jump from high trees to the ground; totally oblivious of the danger. Other times we would slide down very steep, slippery, muddy hills on thin pieces of wood or metal with no way to control how fast we went, grabbing hold of a tree in order to halt our descent before we hit the bottom. When I look back at such times, I thank God that I am alive today.

At home, things like cooking oil and sugar were highly valued, and because they didn't come cheap, my parents ensured that they were used sparingly. Being the mischievous children that we were, whenever my mum went on an errand, my siblings and I would take some maize meal and fry it in a pan with lots of oil and sugar. We would keep stirring the mixture until it hardened. Once ready, the hardened mixture tasted like biscuits. When my mother returned, she would realize that the quantity of sugar and cooking oil had reduced, but when she tried to accuse us of mischief, we would all deny having gone near the valuable commodities. We got so good at convincing her that we were innocent, that she sometimes wondered if her mind was playing tricks on her.

As pre-pubescent girls, trying to make our breasts look bigger was a very popular activity for me and my friends. We would go to such extremes as going down to the river, where a certain kind of insect was found, whose bite caused an itchy swelling. We would then place this insect on our breasts and let it sting us, causing our breasts to swell, making them appear much larger than they really were. The downside to this was the obvious pain that came from the bite and the burning desire to keep scratching our breasts even in public.

My friends and I would also make bras out of banana fiber, cutting the fiber into the desired shape and using ropes and thread to hold the fiber in place. Doing this would make us feel very grown and mature.

Growing up, there was a huge difference between rural and urban set ups in Kenya. After Kenya had won her independence, however, things began to change. African boys and girls now began extending from primary school to high school in huge numbers. Compared to the boys, however, very few girls managed to go to high school in the early post-independence days because most girls would get recruited into secretarial training institutions right out of primary school, from where they would graduate and find employment as secretaries in the city.

The girls that worked in the city would rent rooms during the week. Two or three girls would rent a place together where they worked and would return to the village on the weekends. This was because the distance from the nearest bus stop to our village was a walking distance of about five kilometers on a dusty, unpaved road, so the girls opted to avoid this hustle, and stay in the city.

Whenever these city girls came back to the village, we would always admire them. They would be fashionably dressed in high-heeled shoes and beautiful outfits as well as nice handbags. They would also have shiny afro hair, their lips painted with glossy lipstick and their nails covered with bright nail polish. They also had very smooth and clear skin which we assumed was as a result of the expensive creams and lotions that they used. We always looked forward to the day we would be able to dress and act like them. Every young woman in the village looked up to them as role models, anticipating the day they would have their perceived freedom and independence.

THE INTRICACIES OF LIFE IN THE VILLAGE

Village life was dull and boring with everyone working in their farms from dawn till dusk. As a result, all the young girls would look forward to the weekend when the working girls would return from the city, loaded to the brim with stories of their exciting city adventures. We, the young girls, would sit around them and gaze upon them as if they were princesses, giggling as they spilled the beans on all the mischief they had been up to that week. Of course, they would come bearing strange and exciting tales of city life. The stories would range from simple events that occurred, such as a child falling down a flight of stairs and the drama that unfolded as he was rushed to the hospital. Other stories would be about the new kinds of food they discovered in the city like fish and chips, sandwiches and salads whose names we the village girls could not even pronounce. I remember my older cousin Lucy telling us that in her school she had the choice of having hot or cold lunches. I couldn't for the life of me understand what she was on about. Initially, I thought she would wait for the food to get cold before serving. Later on, I learned that what she referred to as cold lunch were foods such as salads and sandwiches.

The older working girls would also tell us about their thrilling relationships with older men. They boasted about their boyfriends who would take them to concerts and shower them with gifts. We would huddle around them secretly, and they would tell us about their numerous dates with city men, filling our minds with colorful imaginations of being successful and finding rich husbands. They would speak of all the things that young girls are normally curious about. We who were still in the rural areas could not wait for the day we would finish school so that we could get jobs and become like them. As a consequence, many village girls became misinformed. We developed the mentality that the city was the place where you ate life with a big spoon and engaged in all sorts of mischief.

At the same time, there was a concern in the villages that these girls and women who went off to live in the city developed double standards. While they fulfilled their roles as daughters, supporting their parents and siblings back home, they were often thought of as being too independent and exposed to the world and were unlikely to make good wives or even settle down at all. Many men viewed them as poor homemakers.

The daily life in the village was extremely monotonous, and we always looked for ways to keep the days interesting. As my sisters and I grew older, we realized that African girls could straighten their hair. This habit began in the city, and later we, the village girls, were initiated into the practice by the city dwellers. Since we had no access to electricity back in the village, let alone the proper equipment necessary for straightening hair, a friend of ours who lived in the city taught us how to improvise. We would get a small metallic container and hammer holes on its flat bottom surface using nails until it formed a rough, comb-like surface. Red hot charcoal was then carefully poured into the tin which was then used as a makeshift hair dryer.

I will never forget the first time I observed this dangerous process. On that fateful day, my brother was busy straightening my older sister's hair when he accidentally dropped the tin, filled with burning coal onto my sister's shoulders. I remember the horrifying sight of fire all around her shoulders and my poor sister's screams as the hot coal fused with her flesh. It was all very scary and chaotic. It was however unheard of for a girl at the time to be dressed in anything that would expose her body and for that reason, it was easy to keep her burns hidden. We were afraid of what our mother would do if we told her of my sister's unsanctioned attempt at beauty, so instead we decided to keep quiet and watch as my sister suffered in silence.

Our mischief never ceased. One time, I remember secretly sneaking off to Kisumu without my mother's knowledge. My brothers and sisters were all in on the plan to keep my mother in the dark, and I made them promise not to breathe a word of my whereabouts to her until I was safely on the train. I remember pretending that I would be away on a school trip and that I would be back after a night. Despite my assumed accomplished mission, I have long suspected that my mother was well aware of my intentions to spend the night away from home but chose to give me the benefit of doubt.

When I look back at my childhood, I often imagine how sick with worry my siblings and I must have made our mother due to our endless mischief. Our poor mother always had her hand's full keeping tabs on us and to date I am forever grateful for her discipline and hands-on approach in raising her children.

1. Me As a Young Girl at My Childhood Home
2. An Example of the Latrine Toilets in My Primary School
3. My Mother Damaris Nyambura
4. My Father Julius Mukuria
5. My Mother Riding the First Bicycle in the Village
6. My Mother Taking Care of Livestock and My Father on His Way to Work

1. My Parents Standing Next to Our First Car with My Brother Evans in 1968
2. With My Parents
3. The Medical Staff at Kenyatta National Hospital. My father Julius Mukuria is at the Back Row, Third from the Left.
4. My Mother with My Daughter Wandia at her Graduation
5. Front Row L-R: My Sister Sophia Wanjiru, My Mother Damaris Nyambura and My Brother Oscar Machara. Second Row L-R: My Brother Walter Ngaruiya, My Sister Jane Wambui, My Sister Joyce Njeri, Myself, My Brother David Ng'ang'a and My Brother Evans Maruri

PRIMARY AND HIGH SCHOOL

"In school you're taught a lesson and then given a test. In life you're given a test that teaches you a lesson." – Tom Bodett

My earliest memory of life in primary school was that it was a very informal setup. At the time, we were living in reserved villages, which were more like concentration camps, where Africans had been forcefully relocated to after the Mau Mau freedom war began. The villages comprised of an establishment of small, ramshackle dwellings, in which people lived under the watchful eyes of the white settlers. In those days of oppression and war, no funds were allocated for education, and it was up to the villagers to educate their own children.

In 1958, I was awkward beyond belief. I went through much of my primary school life as a lanky girl, resembling a boy and excellently nailed the role of a tomboy. I adored my older brother and his group of male friends. I wanted to be one of the boys, so I followed them everywhere and did the things they did like climbing trees and hunting for wild rabbits that we later roasted over an open fire.

I loved everything the boys did. At school, while other girls giggled and shied away from the teacher's questions, I confidently stood up straight with my answers. As a young girl, I even tucked my dress into my oversized underwear so that I could look like my brother and formed the impression that wearing shorts was all there was to being a boy. I would hang out with them, sitting carelessly with my legs wide apart, chatting and feeling very much like part of the team.

I admired their masculine banter and even took to following my brother into his classroom, despite the fact that he was a grade higher than my own. I looked down on the girls because of how timid they were in class, a fact that perplexed me greatly. I felt at par with the boys and saw them as equals in class and in all other extra-curricular activities. When a boy would hit me, I would not hesitate to hit them right back.

However, even though I was fond of boys, I would always remember my grandmother; her gentle, eloquent voice constantly ringing at the back of my mind about the virtues of womanhood. She was blunt with her words and would constantly warn us about the traps that clever boys lay for 'foolish girls.' Thanks to her loving words of caution, I was keen not to let the boys prey on my body.

I remember the local school as a round hut, where the children would gather with a babysitter, who was usually a teenage girl or adult woman from the village. The children would be grouped together regardless of their age and would spend most of their day at school singing and playing. The children were under no obligation to remain in school if they didn't want to and would go home whenever they felt hungry or got bored.

In what was a makeshift classroom, the children wrote on the earthen floor because they did not have blackboards or any kind of stationary, and of course, they sat on the floor because the school lacked proper desks for the pupils. If anyone wanted a chair to sit on, they would have to bring one from home. It was a very informal setup with no curriculum or trained teachers. Majority of the teachers had not attended school beyond standard two, while others could not even read or write. Many of them were just girls who were only a bit older than the students themselves, and majority never had the chance to attend a proper school.

As young children in the village, we would envy the children who were already attending primary school across the valley. There were no nursery schools for Africans at the time so students would begin school from standard one. The local school at the time only had three classes; standard one up to three, with standard four being introduced later on. In order to further one's education beyond standard four, students had to travel all the way to the neighboring district, which was a very dangerous activity due to the widespread insecurity in the village at the time.

SCHOOL LIFE IN THE 50S'

"No matter who tries to teach you lessons about life, you won't understand it until you go through it on your own"

In the 50s', the Mau Mau war raged on fiercely, and students would sometimes be attacked while making their way to school or back home through the forests. The colonialists were hell-bent on denying Africans any education and they believed that Africans should never rise above becoming supervisors in the various tea or coffee plantations that they owned. As a result, those Kenyans who had been privileged enough to get a proper education outside Kenya came back to the country to teach their fellow countrymen.

By the time I started school myself, the school across the valley had grown, and classes went all the way to standard seven. The events leading up to my starting school were rather strange and unexpected.

My father was the eldest of his parents' children and having been well educated, he had managed to land a good job with an attractive salary. For this reason, his extended family looked to him for all their financial needs, with everyone in my father's family laying claim to his salary and even demanding to be given first priority when it came to how his salary was apportioned.

At one point, my paternal grandmother and my father's sister secretly planned to enroll my auntie's children to school at my father's expense. By chance, one of the teachers at the school happened to know my mother and she told her what was happening behind her back. In a fit of rage and panic, my mother rushed back home that morning, hurriedly shook me out of my slumber and told me that I was going to start school immediately.

For this to happen, I had to pass an interview which involved three stages. In the first stage, I was asked to put my right hand over my head and attempt to touch the lobe of my left ear, a feat which I failed to achieve. The teacher who oversaw this stage knew my mother and wanted to help me get a place in the school so she allowed me to proceed to the next stage. Next, I was asked to write down my parents' name as well as my name on a piece of paper, and finally, I was asked to draw a sketch of anything that came to my mind. I decided to draw an image of three fingers and just like that, I passed the interview. Afterward, the headmistress had a few words with my mother and I was instructed to go into one of the classrooms.

Walking into the classroom, I found children that were much older and bigger than I was. I had never been in such a place and felt very intimidated, so I walked around with my head down and my fingers in my mouth. Because I was very tiny as a child, these students all seemed like giants to me. The boys had on brown Khaki shorts, while the girls wore blue sleeveless dresses with a white blouse. Since most children came from very poor backgrounds, we were allowed to come to school dressed in whatever we wanted to wear, and most of the children had similar outfits with no one's outfit being any better than the other. Sometimes, some of us would come to school in torn clothes or anything that would cover one's body. All the girls had their hair cut short, which was the norm at the school.

Over the next few days, my next-door neighbor also joined the same school, and because we were very good friends, we became inseparable. We did not have a sense of belonging, nor did we concentrate much on our studies. We were very playful and would spend a lot of time playing outside during our breaks and when in class for our lessons, we would anxiously look forward to recess so that we could go and continue our games.

There were only three classrooms in the entire school and the students in Standard one and two would attend school for only half a day. The former in the afternoon and the latter in the morning, which led to them all using the same classroom. Those in standard three and four would attend for a full day so each group had its own classroom.

Most of the children that came from very far would carry something to eat for lunch. They would bring foods like Mandazi, sweet potatoes, and drink tea from a flask. Having a flask meant that you were from a wealthy family. Those who could not afford flasks would carry their tea in plastic or glass bottles, however, most of the children lived close by and therefore went home for lunch. We all could not wait for the day when we would graduate to the upper classes and be able to spend the whole day in school playing with our friends. More than anything, we were excited about the rituals that made up the day-to-day school life; from the sound of the school bell to taking breaks during the day and playing games in the field.

It was all very exciting for us who were new to the school system. Children always looked forward to going home after school so as to show off to the older students who had started school much earlier, that they were now attending school. While we loved going to school so as to avoid all the work our parents made us do at home, we also dreaded it because the teachers were very harsh and would cane the students, sometimes for no reason at all. You would find yourself in trouble for having long and unkempt nails regardless of your gender or sometimes they would ask you to hold up your arm to check whether your armpits were clean and shaven. Brutal caning was the order of the day. Some children feared the cane so much that they would put books and other items underneath their clothes so as to ensure that they did not feel any pain when they were flogged.

Our parents perceived education as the way out of all the difficult troubles and socio-economic problems that we were experiencing during the colonial era. During that time, many Africans believed that education was part of religion and that the two went hand in hand. This was a common misconception which was owed to the fact that it was missionaries who set up the first schools, which they used to spread Christianity. However, as time went by, different groups of people realized the two institutions could exist separately, and that is how schools like

Githunguri high school in Kiambu, which focused mainly on education, sprung up. Most of the people who went there, including my father, wanted to retain their cultural and traditional beliefs while still attaining a Western education.

Part of the education taught in such schools included learning about the political situation in the country and how to govern the country. Schools like Alliance high school, one of the top national schools for boys in the country to this day, firmly believed in teaching education along with religion. They drummed religion into the students and made it compulsory for students to become Christians.

Our parents believed that education was the key to a better life. We all looked forward to leaving rural existence and moving on to something better. We did not have much of a social life, and there were very few entertainment opportunities to take our mind away from our daily routine. We had no televisions and only one radio station broadcasting in the whole country. Things like cassettes came many years later and very few places had radiograms, where you could play different records.

To be able to watch a movie, you would have to go into the city— which was not something that we did on a regular basis—and to do that you had to have a very good reason for it. Going to watch a movie was rare, and of course, the further you lived from the city, the harder it was for you to even dream of going to the city. Movies usually started at 2 PM and ended at 6 PM, which was very late for us children. We would instead choose to entertain ourselves in the vast natural environment that we had at our disposal. We would jump rope, compete in high jump and make contraptions for carrying water with wheels made out of banana fiber. We would also teach our friends all the games we had learned in school.

My early years in primary school are all a bit of a blur; however, I do recall that I was enrolled in a boarding school from standard five. The school called Kalimoni Primary School, located in Juja, Thika, was an all-girls Catholic school that brought together girls from every part of the country with every tribe represented. The beauty of this diversity was that it gave me a chance to interact with children from every corner of the country and to appreciate different cultures.

Later on, when I had the privilege of traveling to Western Kenya during my time in high school, I knew what to expect since I had already familiarized myself with the different tribes and cultures of that part of the country. The student body was divided into day scholars as well as boarders—for those that could afford it.

TRANSITIONING FROM PRIMARY TO HIGH SCHOOL

When I finished my primary school education in 1967, my father tried to get me into a secondary school right next to Kiambu Hospital where he was working at the time. I was put on a waiting list to get into the school and had no hope of joining the school when a friend of my father managed to get me into an Asian school in Nairobi called Khalsa Girls High School simply referred to as Khalsa High, where his daughter was studying.

I immediately enrolled and began attending classes, this time without a "Kipande", an identification tag, around my neck. It had been impossible to visit the city during the imperial days unless you had a tag around your neck and permission from the Home Guards to move around.

The teachers at Khalsa High were very serious and focused on education. This reflected on the performance of the school, which was top notch, and competition among students was very high. Those students who had passed through the corridors of Khalsa High before us had set the bar really high by performing extremely well in their examinations and they had moved on to become successful men and women. The boys especially did very well with some of them going on to start their own industries and companies. The girls, on the other hand, did not seem as successful compared to the boys after they finished school. This was mostly as a result of the cultural belief and norm that girls were supposed to get married immediately after school.

In my first year in high school, I noted that the Indian girls were very bright. They were balanced out in their academics, always doing very well in languages as well as sciences. I also noted that the Indian students were very humble. Were it not for the brand-new school uniforms and expensive lunch boxes carried by some students, you genuinely could not tell the difference between a wealthy student and a student from a poor background.

Most of the African students would carry packed lunch, and they would sit together during breaks to have their meals. It was different for the Indian students because South C, where the school was located, was mainly an Indian estate so they would go home for lunch.

A majority of the African girls were not very focused on their education, and many of them performed very poorly in academics. They would allow themselves to get distracted by African men who would pick them up and take them out for lunch. The girls did everything they could to try and fit in with the city girls and were constantly trying to satisfy their need to have fancy things like perfume, hair products, and makeup. Things that they only dreamed about having while in the village. They knew that the older men would be able to provide these things, and instead of focusing on their education, the young girls chose to spend time with these men so as to get material things in return.

Most of the men were cousins and young uncles to the girls, who would come to see their relatives at school with the sole intention of being introduced to their friends. Once they became acquainted with these men, the girls would then be completely derailed from their educational pursuits. Later on, I learned that most of the men who came to pick up girls at the school gate were family men. I was shocked and very uncomfortable, as I watched my school mates throwing their lives away, all for a bit of fun. These girls focused more on their outward appearance and their dressing than they did on their studies. All they cared about was having fun in the city and getting into relationships with men who were able to show them a good time.

During the period that I studied there, the majority of the school population consisted of Indians. There were few African students and most of them, like the girls who always went for lunches with strange men, were not taken very seriously by the teachers because of their lack of concentration on academic work. The faculty and staff at the school were also mainly composed of Indians. Only the school bazaar and one Swahili teacher were of African descent.

One thing I liked about the school was that once the serious students realized that you were not interested in relationships and city life, they would include you in their study groups. They consequently would invite me to join them in different activities like mathematics competitions and the debate club.

These study groups were very close knit. The girls and boys became more like brothers and sisters and as a result, the boys became very protective of the girls. If a man in the village or from another school tried to harass or seduce one of the girls, for example, the boys would tell him off. Whenever we made trips to other schools for sports competitions or symposiums, the boys would always be close by to ward off any unwanted advances or harassment from students of other schools.

Another thing which led to a lot of the girls getting distracted from their studies was the long journey to school. I remember having to be out of the house as early as 6 AM so as to be in class by 7 AM. The school day ended at 4 PM, and we would end up arriving back home around six o'clock in the evening because of traffic. We would use public means to travel to and fro, and it was here that most girls would be approached by all sorts of men showing their interest in the girls by paying their bus fare and plying them with sweet words. Some girls would not engage in romantic affairs but would spend a lot of their time roaming the town with their friends instead of studying. If they had friends in a nearby school, they would meet up and go to the park to chat and have fun. The day scholars were especially vulnerable to these methods of derailment and distraction.

My high school experience in Nairobi didn't last long. My dad wanted me nearer home and after a year at Khalsa High, I was transferred to a day school called Kahuho High School (Kahuho High) which was a rural government school not far from my parents' home. Kahuho High was built on a hill resting on a five-acre piece of land. The builders had done a good job flattening the steep gradient of the hill to create some sort of playing field for the students.

The classrooms and staff rooms were spread around the school and surrounded by Bougainvillea trees. We didn't have any fences or gates, and you could approach the school compound from any direction. There was a dirt road, however, that vehicles could use to access the school.

My new school was located in the heart of the community. Therefore, if you were a truant and naughty like most of the students at Khalsa High, it did not take long for your family to find out about your behavior because word would reach your parents quickly from the villagers within the community. My older brother and sister had both attended Kahuho High, and here I was, proudly following in their footsteps.

When I started there, I was very happy because it was very close to home. It would take me only a few minutes to walk to school, which I did with a bunch of other students. In those days, cars were rare in the village, and people were used to walking everywhere. We got into a habit of walking together to and from school in a large group. Other village children envied us because we had very smart uniforms which included a gray skirt, a white blouse and a gray sweater with socks and black shoes. Some girls, like me, kept their hair short, although those with long hair kept it very neat and smart. The school was mixed. The interactions between the boys and girls, while strictly monitored by the teachers, went very well.

Although I was disciplined and attentive in class, books and education were not very important to me at this point, save for the Seed of inspiration planted in my mind early on by my father. As much as there was nothing outstanding about my ambitions and aspirations, I was, however, a brilliant young lady. I consequently would effortlessly get way ahead of my classmates in aptitude and grades whenever I chose to apply myself. My mind seemed to work for me and soon, I began to detest all the drill and routine of classroom activity.

By the time I was completing my final term in form one at Khalsa, I had become academically ambitious, and put in extra effort in my classes with the determination to see an improvement in my performance. Slowly I began to see the results of my decision. If for example, we were solving a problem in class, I'd find myself figuring out the solution before the teacher even finished stating the problem. I quickly worked out math quizzes in my head, solving each problem before my classmates. During classes, I'd listen to the teacher for only a few minutes, then switch to think about something else and catch up with the learning later. It didn't matter what subject it was, they were all equally easy to me, and I soon became bored of the pace of learning.

DARING TO SUCCEED

"Life is either a daring adventure or nothing"

By my second year in high school, I was fed up with the slow pace with which my teachers were covering the syllabus, so I decided to stop attending classes completely. In order to get myself out of class without raising any eyebrows, I lied to the school administration that my parents were having financial problems and could not afford to pay my school fees. At home, I made sure I maintained my normal routine, pretending to go to school early in the morning and coming home at a suitable time. In this way, I was able to fool both sides.

Prior to the decision I made to stop attending classes, I had spoken to the teachers in order to find out how much of the syllabus they expected to have covered by the end of the term. Once I completed making my inventory of what I needed to learn, I went off to study on my own. I identified a lonely, hidden spot in the countryside where I would go to study. Every day I woke up and went through the motions of getting ready for school, then left home taking my books and everything I needed in a basket. I then went off to my hiding spot or some other quiet place to study. At the time, it was very common for students to miss school due to lack of school fees. The teachers would not question when a student was absent and as a result, I absconded school for a whole term and only reported back when we were about to sit for the end of term examinations.

It is important to note that my father Mr. Julius Ng'ang'a, had studied for his A-level exams on his own, thus becoming one of the few self-taught Kenyans to make it through high school in the '40s. He sat for his exams alongside the candidates of Alliance High School, where he did extremely well and went on to enroll at a medical college. I was literally living up to my father's high standards and following in his footsteps, albeit in a secretive and aberrant way. My parents thought I went to school every morning when I made off with my books and lunch for the day, yet my teachers thought I had dropped out for lack of school fees.

When I got back to school to sit for my examinations, I noticed to my great joy that in all the papers I sat for, I had the answer to a majority of the questions asked, including in the subjects I had previously struggled with. It was very clear in my mind that I had done very well in the examination even before I received my results.

I remember one morning just before the results of the exams were due to be released, the principal called me to his office and asked me to clear my fees so they could let me know what my results were and my position in the class. I quickly replied that I already knew I had done very well and was probably in the top five. Please note then I was not an A student and my results typically came back average. However, I strongly believed that my determination to work harder than all the other students, even though I was no longer getting any guidance from the teachers would indeed make me perform well in class. The principal surprised by the accuracy of my statement, enquired if I had been given this information by a teacher because as it turned out, I was the first not only in my class but in the three form two streams. I was very excited to find out that I was top in all the subjects other than physics and chemistry.

When I took my results home, my family was elated and none the wiser. At that moment, I realized that it was not the teacher's input that was important, but one's own individual effort and discipline in their studies. The teachers in the school were very surprised and shocked to see how well I performed, given that I had missed a whole term of school. Even the Asian students, who believed Africans could not perform well in academia, were very impressed. I immediately became popular with them, and most of the students started getting closer to me and wanted to be associated with me.

I attended Kahuho High for the remainder of my high school years. To keep myself busy and distracted from the school routine that I was now accustomed to, I decided to join different clubs. One of the clubs I remember joining was the debate club. Although I did not actively participate because the boys were very domineering and hogged the stage and the discussions, I enjoyed sitting at the back of the classroom watching them deliberate over the different issues that were presented. Life was largely unexciting until my final year when a strange group of tourists visited our school and my life took on a whole new twist.

THE BEGINNING OF MY INCREDIBLE LIFE JOURNEY

"You have to take risks. We will only understand the miracle of life fully when we allow the unexpected to happen." – Paulo Coelho

One afternoon seated in the back row of the little noisy school hall, my friends and I waited anxiously for the next debate club session to begin. That day, feeling very tired from the hot sun outside, I didn't clamor for a chance to contribute to whatever the debate was about. I sat next to the window with half an ear to the heckling in the room, while the rest of my mind and eyes roamed around outside through the open window, staring into the blue sky.

Suddenly, something caught my eye. It was a convoy of about six vans slowly making its way into the school compound, all branded with UTC in bold letters. At the time, this was the most popular 'Tours and Travel' company in Kenya. All the vans were painted in black and white zebra stripes. They had open roofs from where I could see white people peering from and taking pictures. To a village girl who rarely ever saw white people, the sight looked like something out of a movie.

My school was located in a very remote part of the village and to get there, you had to travel along a very rough dirt road, so we rarely received any visitors, let alone white tourists. It was all very strange and new to me. I wondered how on earth they had ended up in my school. I assumed that they must have wanted to see what African schools looked like, and their guide decided to bring them to my school.

The activities in our little debate hall had now been disrupted by the approaching entourage, and everyone was abuzz with excitement. The vans slowly came to a halt in the middle of the school compound, and the driver of the lead vehicle went around his van to open the door for his strange passengers. I held my breath in anticipation, craning my neck and widening my eyes, waiting to see who our strange guests were. My eager eyes were not disappointed as out of the vehicle emerged a man and a woman; two of the whitest people I had ever seen!

Since I was known to be very humorous and courageous, I casually turned to my friends and said "I think these definitely look like my guests, let me go and say hello", and everyone started laughing. No African child would have dared to approach white strangers riding in a strange van, but they all guessed Wanjiku could, which to their amusement, I did. My friends thought I was just overstretching one of my jokes as usual, but to their amazement, I walked right up to the visitors and chatted with them while the whole school stared in awe. The tourists were very excited to see me, and they greeted me warmly while introducing themselves as Mr. George and Mrs. Irene Kraft. They appeared extremely white and pale to me, as though they had never been exposed to the sun. They then began to ask me all sorts of questions about myself and my school while taking pictures of me.

My previous encounter with a white person was during the colonial era, and even then, I could only stare at them from afar. We were not allowed to have any direct communication with them, so this was the first time I got to speak directly to a white person. At the time, my impression of the white man was that they were brutal and oppressive and as they continued to speak to me, I stood there, flabbergasted, staring at them without uttering a word. They then asked me if I could sing and since I was not one to back out of a challenge, I proceeded to sing the national anthem which of course, I knew quite well.

In no time, the whole school had gathered around us, my fellow students giggling and laughing as our strange guests continued to take more pictures. After speaking with me for a little while, Mr. and Mrs. Kraft asked if I had any friends and I immediately called out one of my best friends from the crowd. We put our arms around each other's shoulders as friends do, as the tourists took pictures of us smartly dressed in our uniforms. After a brief tour of the school, the group of tourists bade us farewell and climbed aboard their open roofed vans. There was so much excitement in the school that the teachers had a hard time getting everyone back into class. Little did I know that this short stint at the school with the American strangers was forever going to change my life.

"Don't be afraid to take risks, for they make life worth living"

A few weeks after the Krafts had left for America, they mailed the pictures of that day to me through the school's post office box. During that time, there was only one post office box with the address PO Box 79 Kabete, which was shared by the entire village. The same box was also used by the only church in the village as well as the primary school. To receive mail, one had to take the long walk to Lower Kabete town from Cura village.

When the pictures from the Krafts were delivered to the school. Word traveled quickly that I had received a package from America, and the whole school trooped to my desk after class to gaze at the pictures. These were the first color pictures my schoolmates, and I had ever seen. It was such a big deal seeing ourselves in full color, next to these strange white people.

In a letter that they had stashed in an envelope within the pictures, they took time to tell me more about themselves. I was fascinated to find out that George Kraft was an American orthopedic surgeon, while Irene, his wife, was a Norwegian who worked as a nurse in the US. They asked me to write back to them which I did with so much excitement and from then onwards we began a back and forth correspondence.

I remember that I initially found it difficult to understand the writing in their letters and some phrases that they would use were sometimes difficult to decipher as I was not used to American English. Sometimes, I would consult my older cousin to understand what the letters meant. Later I decided to change my address from the school address to my home address where all the family mail would be received. This was easier for me because I didn't have to endure questions from my friends and teachers at school about my dealings with the Krafts. Also, my father's cousin worked at the post office, and he would bring us our mail every other week. This arrangement was wonderful for me because it meant that I didn't have to walk all the way to the post office to get the mail myself.

In their correspondence, the Krafts were very interested to know what my future plans were and what profession I wanted to pursue after high school. They wanted to know how I wanted to achieve my dreams and if I had any intentions of traveling abroad to study. Finally, they asked me if I would be interested in furthering my education in America and without knowing what it entailed I enthusiastically said yes.

My back and forth correspondence with the Krafts went on unhindered for a while until my father's cousin from the post office went on leave from work for one month. At the time, any letters belonging to members from the village were collected by the church and kept until Sunday. The mail was then distributed during the church service and members of the congregation were called to the front to collect their respective letters.

With my contact at the post office now on leave, I had to decide to either wait until Sunday or make my way to a town called Kangemi, a long walk from my village to collect the letters myself. Little did I know that my regular visits to the mailbox had caught the eye of the postmaster, a thirty-something-year-old man who had it in his head that he could have his way with me.

The man began to try and make idle conversation every time I showed up. He had figured out that the letters were very dear to me, and he used this to try and win my affection. I realized that telling him off would most likely jeopardize me receiving any letters; so instead, I tried as much as I could to be nice to him.

Sometimes he would invite me to his house, put on some music on his radiogram and try to get me to dance with him. He played Jim Reeves and all those melancholic tunes of the seventies, but I fell for none of his tricks. However, I did my best to politely turn down his distasteful advances as I didn't want him to hide my letters out of spite. When he realized, I was unyielding to his seduction, he then changed his tactics and began to boast about his importance at the post office to impress me. I decided to stay away from the post office for a while as I pondered on what to do about the situation. Luckily, my father's cousin who used to bring us our mail returned to work from his leave, and I was thrilled because I did not have to return to the post office anymore.

PREPARING FOR AMERICA: FROM THE VILLAGE TO LOS ANGELES

"Dare to live the life you have dreamt for yourself"

In the time between 1969 and 1972, the Krafts managed to secure an admission for me into the California State University. Everything was happening so quickly, and one particular area that I needed consultation in was with regard to getting my visa. In my naivety, I thought a visa was something the Krafts were going to send via cable or something like a telegram. On finding out this was not the case, I decided to consult with my cousin, who became curious about my correspondence with the Krafts. He became even more inquisitive, wanting to know who the Krafts were and how I met them. I was suspicious of his curiosity and decided not to let him see their address in case he decided to communicate with them directly.

After I realized that the Krafts were serious about their intention to fly me to America, I approached my parents and told them about this exciting opportunity. While my father was surprised to learn that the Krafts were not just mere pen pals, my mother was very wary about sending me away to a foreign land for several years, all by myself.

At the time, African people were distrusting of the white man and how they treated African women. Before independence, many black women were raped and mistreated, and the misconception of the white man continued to hang heavy on the African mind more so my parents. It took much convincing and dialogue before everyone was on board with the idea.

The Krafts sent over all the documents from the university, showing that they had indeed secured a place for me at the school. This seemed to somewhat ease my parents' concern although I could tell they were still experiencing mixed feelings. On one hand, they were excited for the grand opportunity that lay before me; on the other, caution and the fear of the unknown made them cringe at the thought of letting me go.

As much as I dreaded leaving my home, friends, and family, I didn't think I would miss my lifestyle much because to me, growing up on a farm was akin to torture. Every day we worked from dawn to dusk and got to eat the same food day in day out. If we weren't having boiled sweet potatoes or githeri which consisted of a mixture of maize and beans, then it was ugali made from flour and water or mukimo made out of mashed greens and potatoes. We would only break this monotonous diet cycle during Christmas, a time that we definitely looked forward to.

I was extremely happy about the opportunity that lay ahead of me, but as reality sunk in, a dull, sad feeling began to creep into my heart. I began to realize that I was going away for a very long time, and it would be years before I would set foot on my mother land. I realized that I would not be able to see my family and my friends until I finished college. Whenever I had a meal, regardless of how tasteless it might be,

I would savor every bite I took, because I knew that pretty soon I would not be able to taste my African delicacies even if I wanted to.

I was excited about leaving the country and learning about different cultures and meeting with different kinds of people. There had been women from our village who had traveled out of the country, only to come back looking very changed with very beautiful skin that had become several shades lighter and I imagined that the same would happen to me.

Once it was established that I would go to the United States to further my education, my parents began preparing for the journey. They started by seeking out anyone from the village who had traveled by plane to America in order to prepare me for anything I needed to know about my travel and the airport processes, as well as what to expect once I arrived there. The resident expert on all matters of travel was Mr. Kamuria. Even though he had only flown once— traveling to Britain for a conference— everyone considered him to be the village travel guru.

I remember him narrating a dramatized story about his journey to Britain. My parents and I all sat in silence as we carefully listened to his vivid tale. He explained that once I was on the plane, I would meet stewards and hostesses who would all be clad in white, assuming that they would all have the same dress and color code for every airline. He continued to explain that they would let me know the different meal options served on the plane and that they would continue to serve us as we remained seated. He mentioned that they would be in charge of security on the flight, and I would have to wear a belt which was meant to keep me in my chair. As he told us of the experience that lay ahead of me, he would act out all that he said with hand gestures, tonal variations, and facial expressions, making the story very dramatic. This, in turn, fueled my eagerness and excitement even more.

My family, on the other hand, reassured themselves that although I would be gone for a long time, we would ultimately see each other again once my studies were complete. Despite this, some family members would continue to remind me not to forget them, while others would write me notes subtly warning me not to forget my culture and traditions and become like the white people in that new land.

A few days later, my parents began planning my farewell party which was to be held on the afternoon of my departure. All the village folk were invited. My father chose a fattened goat and set it aside for the celebration, as my mother went about tidying up the homestead and preparing for the visitors. My father had also hired a bus, which would be used to ferry the villagers who would escort me to the airport, as well as a small saloon car in which I would travel.

On the day of the party, my father and a few of the village men woke up very early and slaughtered the goat; while my mother, along with my siblings and a few women, began to prepare the food. Everything was ready by midday, just as the visitors began to arrive. We had a merry time eating and celebrating, and I remember tears flowing down my face at the love the villagers showed me as they showered me with blessings and kind words wishing me well on my new journey. After a few speeches and a word of prayer, the party was over and it was time to make our way to the airport. A large group of villagers were packed tightly into the 29-seater minibus and I recall the bus was so full that I wondered if it would make it to the airport and back in one piece.

I, however, did not travel in the bus. This was due to the superstition by the village folks that anyone traveling was in need of protection from people who did not wish them well or anyone who did not want them to go away for whatever reason. For girls especially, it was feared that there might be a man who had a romantic interest in them, and he might try to prevent her from traveling by kidnapping her or harming her in some way. For that reason, I sat in the small saloon car with my parents and a trusted family member.

The car I was in led the way, with an experienced driver guiding us through Nairobi city, to the Jomo Kenyatta International Airport. The bus followed closely, filled to the brim with excited villagers. Coming from a village with no electricity and houses made of mud and grass thatched roofs, no one wanted to miss this great opportunity to see the tall city buildings, the city center lights and the planes at the airport. In those days, terrorism was unheard of, and everyone could come and go into and from the airport as they pleased.

Once at the airport, Mr. Kamuria handed me a white handkerchief. I was supposed to use it to wave goodbye to my friends when I got in line to board the plane. After going through security and checking in for my flight, I proceeded to the plane and as expected turned to wave goodbye to my friends and family. They were all standing at a waving bay area waving frantically while shouting their goodbyes.

I was traveling with Trans World Airlines, the only airline company at the time to make direct flights from Nairobi to the United States. People would just refer to it as TWA and to the wide-eyed girl that I was, it all sounded very exciting.

When I got on the plane, I made sure to follow the instructions I had been given by our resident travel expert back in the village and as the plane took off, I was filled with overwhelming anxiety knowing that my chance to make something of myself and to experience a new adventure had come. Due to all the excitement I was feeling, I stayed awake throughout the entire journey even though it was a twenty-two-hour direct flight to New York with a one-hour transit before boarding another connecting flight to Los Angeles.

1. The Entrance to Cura Primary School
2. One of the Primary School Classrooms
3. A View of Cura Primary School after the Classrooms Were Built
4. With a Friend the late Minnie Ngingi at Kahuho High School
5. With and a Friend I Met During the Trip to Kakamega Where I had Travelled Without My Mum's permission.

1. My Friend and I Outside the School Classes And on Our First Meeting with Doctor Kraft
2. Standing next to a UTC bus parked at the Nairobi International Showground in 1970
3. With My Boyfriend from Nairobi
4. The Signs and Pathway Leading To the ACK Church
5. A Current Picture of the ACK Church

CHASING MY AMERICAN DREAM

"You have to dream hard, wish big and chase after your goals because no one else is going to do it for you"

When I finally touched down at the Los Angeles International Airport, the night was just beginning to set in. After I had gone through airport security and the customs section, I was overjoyed to see Mr. and Mrs. Kraft waiting for me with huge smiles on their faces.

The Krafts were just as warm and receptive as the day I had met them back at my school. As soon as they saw me, they both walked over to give me a huge hug which I found quite strange. Back home, people never showed affection in that manner and for a moment, I was confused and didn't know how to respond.

As soon as we got my luggage, we headed to the parking lot. I was amazed to see all kinds of beautiful cars, some that I had never seen in my life. We walked up to an elegant brown Cadillac, and Mr. Kraft lifted my suitcase into the boot which he referred to as "trunk".

In all my life in the village, I had never seen such a car before. It was very wide and spacious, and I was shocked to see windows moving up and down at the touch of a button. As we drove down the streets through the city, I was in complete awe; staring out at the city lights which went on for as far as the eyes could see, up and down the undulating gradients of the land. I marveled at the sight of tall buildings that seemed to reach the sky, six-lane highway and beautiful cars cruising past. Seeing this for the first time was indeed a jaw dropping experience.

The Krafts were good, jolly people and they made my arrival a memorable experience with their bright, welcoming smiles and endless queries about my trip as well as my home. We drove past picture-perfect estates until we got to their neighborhood in Woodland Hills in San Fernando Valley in Los Angeles County. When we arrived at their house, I was amazed to see the gates and the garage doors opening automatically. As we parked the car and walked into the house, I remember being fascinated by everything I saw and heard. Here I was at this place where everything was completely different; where the doors opened automatically, and all was extremely clean. It seemed like I was in some sort of paradise and not in an actual house.

The interior of the house looked extremely clean, almost as if no one had ever set foot in it before. Everything in it was neat and exquisite. A white, fluffy carpet covered the entire living room floor. There were gold covers and beautiful furnishings everywhere, with large colorful paintings hanging on the walls. Colorful wallpaper spanned the walls and elegant chandeliers hung from the high ceiling above. The bathrooms were spectacular; spotless and sparkling, with beautiful towels and furnishings.

Everything appeared brand-new, and I felt out of place walking about in the faded dress I was wearing.

I neither had the experience of having a telephone in my house nor had I ever encountered a speaking clock or a popcorn machine. The bedroom, the porch, the garden, the pavements, swimming pool and everything else was just magnificent. Life seemed to have turned upside down, and my jaw was on the floor the whole time.

I was ushered into this huge room and told it was going to be my bedroom. There was a huge TV, and I was amazed to find out that it was meant just for me. The bed was very well made, with beautiful, matching bedspreads. My room had its own bathroom which was cleaner and more magical than anything I had seen before.

Mrs. Kraft then asked me if I would prefer to take a bath or a shower and for a moment I was quite confused since I did not understand what a shower was. Back in the village, bathrooms were little wooden stalls located outside the main house and one had to fetch water in a basin or a bucket and carry it into the little room to have a wash. Having the privilege to choose between hot and cold water just by turning handles was very complicated, and I remember struggling to use it for some time as I was not used to washing so lavishly.

Mrs. Kraft continued to slowly explain how the different automated systems and electronics in the house worked. I was amazed to learn that machines could actually wash clothes and dishes as well as dry them, and I wondered how this was possible. I had always thought that water damaged electrical items, and I wondered how this machine would work without getting damaged.

After the brief tour of what seemed to me like a mansion, Mrs. Kraft offered me a drink. I wondered if I should ask for a glass of water, but instead ended up asking for Treetop; a popular brand of juice that I had grown up drinking.

Of course, they did not know what I was talking about so they opted to give me choices of different juices instead, asking which one I would prefer. I had never heard of any of the flavors they described and became visibly confused, which prompted Mrs. Kraft to choose a flavor that she thought I might like: chilled freshly squeezed orange juice which she served in a tall glass.

Feeling exhausted I decided to retire to my room and have an early night. I lay out my suitcase on my bed and stood, still gazing at my entire Kenyan life all packed up in one tiny box. My mom had made me two dresses which I had packed with the only sweater I owned.

Everything in my little suitcase seemed so out of place and worn out compared to the luxury of my new accommodation. Feeling anxious and overwhelmed with emotion, I got into my new bed. I remember sleeping so well that night, feeling like I was lying on a bed of feathers. As excited as I was to finally begin chasing my dream, I could not help but think about my family back home. All my siblings sharing a single bed, all sleeping under the one roof which made up our entire house.

The next morning, I was gently stirred from my dreams by beautiful melodic chimes from a huge grandfather clock that stood majestically in the living room. The Krafts had a very small dog, which came running into my room and started barking at me, jumping all over the bed. I wondered if it was really a dog because it was so tiny and almost resembled a fluffy doll. Back home, dogs were huge and fierce and they certainly were never allowed to come into the house. I sat on the edge of the bed without a clue on how to handle this tiny fluffy creature.

On my first morning at the Krafts breakfast table, I was presented with a wide variety of food items to choose for breakfast. From different kinds of cereal, bread, to various other foods that I was not familiar with such as croissants and marmalade. Mrs. Kraft placed the cereal on the table with milk and some sugar. Since I truly had no idea what to do with either milk or sugar, I settled on simple bread with what appeared to be margarine, which I was more familiar with. Mrs. Kraft was, however, very patient with me. She slowly explained how to mix the milk and sugar with the cereal and suggested for me to try out the jam and marmalade.

We continued to engage in conversation and excitedly, the Krafts began to break down the activities they had planned for the day and the different places they could not wait to take me. I struggled to understand most of what they were saying because their accent sounded different from the English that was spoken back in the village, and I often found myself smiling and nodding my head in agreement at anything they would ask.

After breakfast, I continued to tour the other part of the house. Having left my tiny house in Cura village where I shared a bedroom with three of my sisters, I couldn't help but feel excited watching my life immediately begin to change in front of my eyes.

ADJUSTING TO LIFE IN AMERICA

"In the end we only regret the chances we did not take"

I stayed with the Krafts for three months, as I waited to join University later that year. During my three-month stay, they got me a job as a cleaner in a doctor's office. This job was very odd to me because I could not understand what they wanted me to clean since everything appeared spotless and without a trace of dust or dirt. I however appreciated the opportunity to work there as I began to learn a great deal about Americans and their culture.

The 70s were years of fads and fashion in America. The country was on a fantasy trip to Nirvana. The women began to wear miniskirts and high-heeled platform shoes, while the men began to dress in bell bottom pants and hip huggers – also wearing platform shoes as high as that the ladies would wear.

Both the men and women were donning large hairstyles, with the Afro being the extremely popular hairstyle of the 70s, particularly among the African Americans. The magazines became glossier and there was partying, music, and dancing everywhere you looked. The most popular genre of music at the time was rock and disco.

Musicians like Bob Marley began to gain huge scores of fans in the United States with his reggae vibes. The Beatles, the Bee Gees, Elvis Presley and Elton John were massively popular. This was also the era when Carl Bernstein wrote the book All the President's Men. Big spending, fine living, and marijuana was also the highpoint of American life. Everybody was smoking cannabis, and it was normal to see people—including mature women—rolling marijuana cigarettes and passing on the rolls like you would a normal cigarette.

I got into none of that and maintained a simple, controlled lifestyle that saw me escape the trap of America's excesses. I had never seen such contrasts in lifestyle, technology, and behavior. Even the little things in American life seemed exaggerated and blown up to me. Nothing made sense, and I felt far too removed from the real world as I knew it.

The Krafts had warned me against talking to strangers. In my free time, I learned to love dogs, ride a bike, and embrace strange practices like undressing on the beach while changing into a swimming costume.

All these were very different from what I was used to in my culture, and it took almost two years for me to adapt to America's outrageous ways.

Before I left Kenya, the Krafts and I had discussed that I would make my academic course selections once I got to the United States. I arrived in the middle of the academic year, and because I could not embark on my degree right away, I enrolled part-time at a local college where I took some courses to familiarize myself with American English as a second language.

This also gave me the opportunity to learn about different cultures while interacting with people from all walks of life. We had also agreed that when I settled down and knew my way around, I would move from the Krafts' household to live with another family who was much closer to the university so I would not have to spend hours commuting to and from school.

After three months, I moved as agreed and went to stay with a Jewish woman named Florence, who had a 17-year-old son. Florence was a 45-year-old divorcee and was preparing to marry again. I remember her house was so big that you could have played soccer in the living room.

As preparations for the wedding got under way, Florence decided to get a face-lift to improve her looks. I accompanied her for the operation, and when she emerged from surgery, her face was swathed in bandages. She asked me to move into her bedroom during her recovery so as to help her with anything she might need as she recuperated from surgery.

In about a week she had recovered, looked years younger than her actual age of 45. I later learned that plastic surgery was a common practice in America and that one of her neighbors also had an 18-year-old brother who underwent plastic surgery in order to change the shape of his nose.

People in America changed their looks as much as their clothing just to suit the occasion. Whenever I went out, Florence would always advise me on how to match my clothes. It was frowned upon to throw on whatever you felt like, however comfortable you felt in it. Colors were supposed to match, and one had to ensure that your clutch or handbag also matched with your shoes and outfit.

This was definitely very new to me since back in the village putting on any piece of clothing just to cover up your body was the order of the day. I came to learn about things like deodorants, perfumes, facial creams, mouth sprays, and other makeup essentials that were mandatory for ladies. I genuinely began to wonder how my friends and I had survived all those years with soap and water as our daily essentials.

One day, on a snowy winter's evening, I attended a dance in the neighborhood in a sleeveless dress that I had carried to the United States with me. It was made by my tailor in the village and I matched it with a black handbag, brown earrings, and a necklace. Before we left for the dance, a friend of mine, dressed in jeans, a hat, and jacket with closed shoes, asked me if I was sure I would be comfortable in my sleeveless dress. It was freezing cold outside and she was concerned that I would catch a cold or worse just by exposing myself to these unbearable temperatures. I assured her that I would be fine. I thought that it was important for me to look my best at the dance and I figured that I would brave the weather. At the dance, everybody kept staring at me which made me feel somewhat uneasy. It did not cross my mind that they were probably perturbed by my choice of dressing, and instead thought that they were staring at me because I was a foreigner and a visitor in America.

Later in the night when I got home, I found Florence in the living room. She immediately began to scold me for dressing like that in the middle of winter and leaving the house without wearing a coat. I was confused and instead felt that Florence and the other people at the dance did not understand my Kenyan look or my attempt to mix and match the different colors in my outfit.

As time went on and other, I realized that I didn't understand the American people, just as much as they failed to understand me. They had their culture and tradition, just as I had my own, and only time would tell if I would embrace them and if we would ever understand each other's diversities.

UNIVERSITY AND CHASING AFTER THE AMERICAN DOLLAR

"You have to take risks. We will only understand the miracle of life fully when we allow the unexpected to happen". – Paulo Coelho

Days turned into months and still I continued to struggle to fit in with these people who all seemed completely crazy in the way they talked and acted. Vehicle horns blared in the streets during the day and club music filled the air at night. It was almost too overwhelming for me and at times I found myself wishing that I had never left my safe, quiet village.

It was as if the world was spinning too fast and I could barely keep up with life in America. My situation was worsened by the fact that I had no one to confide in—no one from my motherland to explain what America was all about.

The summer before I joined the university, I attended evening classes which were specifically to help me understand the American accent. I was trying my best to blend in and I believed if I could at least speak like an American I would feel like I belong. I looked forward to Saturday mornings when I would get to visit and spend time with the Krafts.

I would wake up very early in the morning and catch the two-hour bus ride which would drop me off at Dr. Kraft's office. We had agreed that I would be spending my Saturday mornings cleaning and arranging his office so as to earn some extra money which would help with my expenses. I would take about two hours and once I was done he would pay me $20, which at the time was quite a lot of money for the amount of work done. Dr. Kraft always had my best interests at heart and tried to do what he could to support my education.

Once I was done, we would then leave and go spend the afternoon with Mrs. Kraft at their lovely house. She was always excited to see me and would welcome me with delightful snacks like apple pies and fresh croissants.

As much as I enjoyed sharing my stories with the Krafts about my week and updating them on my day-to-day life living with Florence, there was still a void in my heart that I was yearning to fill. Even though it had been months already since I landed in the United States, welcomed by the Krafts with my tiny suitcase, it felt as though I was still struggling to fit in.

I remember one time, during a dinner that I had been invited to, a boy came up to me and asked if I would dance with him. I politely declined, expecting him to charm me into submission. You see, back home, girls were expected to resist any attempt at courtship by the boys. As their advances were turned down, the boys would in turn charm the girls until they agreed to dance with them. This time, however, when I declined the American boy's offer to dance, he just shrugged and walked away. I was left feeling perplexed and a bit offended by his actions.

My friend, seated right next to me, noticed my disappointment when the boy walked away and whispered that I had nothing to worry about and that the boy had no other intentions than to have just one dance with me. He wasn't courting me or offering to become my friend and all you wanted was one dance. As expected this was very strange to me.

Every day I woke up to new aspects of the American culture that I had not encountered before. Girls there seemed to be too reckless and free with boys. I was constantly surprised to see people kissing on the streets in broad daylight. My American friends went out all night on dates with their boyfriends, with the full permission of their parents which to me was completely absurd.

One evening, during my stay with Florence, a friend of mine from the neighborhood invited me out for dinner with her parents and her sister. As we ate and talked, my friend suddenly announced that her boyfriend had invited her for a weekend trip and asked me to come along. She went on to explain that her boyfriend would bring his friend, another boy to keep me company, so I would not be lonely.

As the words continued to pour out of her lips, my heart was in my mouth. I could not believe she was saying these things right in front of her parents. Back home, such a discussion would never have occurred within an earshot of my parents.

As I sat there, frozen, waiting for some kind of outburst from her parents, I was surprised when her mother merely smiled and agreed with her daughter, saying that she was sure I would enjoy the experience. Her father even asked me how I felt about the idea of going away with a boy for the weekend. I could only nod with a half-smile on my lips. I was at a complete loss for words.

Back in the village, girls were instructed from an early age to always be on their guard when socializing with boys because they were always up to some mischief. Hence, when my friend and I went for the weekend trip, I was wary of the two boys for fear of being tricked into something— now more than ever, stories from my grandmother about clever men destroying naive girls' futures seemed very real. At one point on the trip, the boy I was with tried to help me take off my jacket at the dinner table, but I politely turned him down. I was determined to keep my distance from him at all costs.

To my surprise, when we got back home, the first thing my friend's mother asked was if we enjoyed ourselves. Enjoyed? I sat there wondering what she meant by 'enjoyed.' Meanwhile, my friend was excitedly narrating every little detail about our experience to her parents.

When it was my turn to share my experience, I was at a loss for words knowing that if it were my parents, the discussion would never have come up in the first place. My friend on the other hand continued to share different stories from the weekend, including letting her parents know that she could tell that the guy I was with really liked me—all this from the look on his face. I felt so embarrassed and shy at the same time. All I could do was gaze at the floor and blush.

That weekend made me realize that in America, spending time with a boy didn't mean that he was courting you, nor did it mean that he was out to trick you into something you didn't want to do. It was simply two people enjoying each other's company. I began to wonder about my own culture and why women were taught that men were always up to no good and hence constantly encouraged to stay away from them. My experience in America made me realize that I should think otherwise. I began to realize that how one's life turned out was based on one's individual decisions and discipline, not rules and traditions which only control our thoughts and behavior because it is perceived as "socially acceptable".

One evening, I visited my friend again at her home. When she opened the door, I immediately noticed that she had been crying. At the sight of me, she burst out tearfully and put her arms around my neck in some kind of embrace. When I asked her what the matter was, she tried to speak, but just broke down in tears, sobbing uncontrollably.

I entered their living room and saw that her mother and sister were crying, too. My first thought was that some misfortune might have happened to their dad since he was the only one not in the room at the time. As I sat there wondering what might have happened to him, he walked out of one of the bedrooms. I let out a sigh of relief when I spotted him, but I was instantly confused again because he too seemed sad and somber.

Then he broke the news to me. "Scooby is dead," he said. "She died this morning."

Scooby? I wondered who in the world that was, as my mind raced, trying to merge a face with the name. Then, after a few seconds, I suddenly remembered that Scooby was the name of their dog. I was slightly confused when I realized that the family was mourning the passing of a dog.

My friend's father announced that he would make funeral arrangements as soon as Scooby's cause of death was declared. "Funeral arrangements and post mortems for pets?" I thought quietly to myself. I could not believe how pampered American pets were and struggled to contain my emotions.

The fact that there were sections in the supermarket with food just for dogs or cats was something I had never imagined possible. It was some sort of paradise where people always had enough food and pets were treated as members of the family. When all I knew were veterinary doctors for cows, in America it was not strange to take a dog to see a veterinary doctor.

Sometimes they would be taken for pampering sessions where they would get their hair cut or teeth checked. Memories of the old Bedford stretcher and the deep, wide mass graves of days gone by flooded my mind. I remembered the many dogs and cats, which had been hit and killed by speeding motorists back in Kenya, and left to rot by the roadside with nobody to mourn for them. Life here seemed unreal and the culture never ceased to baffle me.

In my opinion, Americans were very strange people who lived in a strange world without rules and chose to do whatever they liked. Village life was the complete opposite. The villagers were grouped into clans and age sets; everyone had a role and duty to fulfill in the community. I was mortified to see men who dressed up like women, holding hands, and appearing to be intimate with each other. The women, too, engaged in relationships with other women. I had never encountered homosexuals and cross-dressers before and was therefore greatly perplexed by this phenomenon. I also learned about strange diseases and strange medical terminology which I never encountered before.

Terms like psychoanalysts, alcoholism, counselors, and family therapists sounded strange and exotic to me and I wondered when I would finally get to embrace this American culture.

LEARNING TO COPE IN
THE AMERICAN JUNGLE

Every day was as shocking and fast-paced as the day I arrived. The technology though undoubtedly impressive, constantly baffled me as everything seemed to be computerized or operated by push-button mechanisms.

My crazy culture shock continued right into my college years. During my freshman year, I decided to go shopping to buy a few clothes and supplies. I ended up wondering into a department store that had just opened near campus.

Back home in the Indian shops, you could bargain for nearly any commodity that was up for sale. So when I spotted a $3 handbag that I really liked, I happily picked it off the shelf and joined the express checkout queue ready to negotiate the price of the handbag down to $2. When it was my turn to pay at the counter, I asked the lady cashier whether she could bring the price down to $2.

Needless to say, I was not ready for her reaction. She became furious and asked me why I had bothered to pick up the bag in the first place if I couldn't afford it. As I tried to explain myself, people in the queue behind me started getting restless, and some began shouting for me to hurry up, as they did not have "all day to stand there."

Realizing that the situation was getting out of hand, the cashier took me aside and reported me to her manager, who was equally as cold. In the end, I was forced to pay full price for the bag. I stormed out of the store furious and crushed. Hot tears streamed down my eyes as I walked back home. I genuinely failed to grasp why I had to pay the full three dollars for the bag despite my pleas to the Manager that I did not have enough money. In my mind, this was a great injustice.

Soon, the money I had saved up while working as a cleaner at the doctor's office had run out. Since I was on a partial scholarship, I had no other choice but to look for a job in order to earn a living and pay my tuition fees.

Someone mentioned to me that jobs including nurses and medical assistants were always plentiful in America and could easily be found advertised in the newspapers. I, unfortunately, did not have any experience to apply as a nurse or as a medical assistant.

Instead, I quickly managed to get a housekeeping job.

I decided to buy a bicycle which I would use to get to work since the house was quite far from where I lived. After looking at a few bikes in different shops, I found one that I liked and paid a whopping $25.

On the day I was due to begin my housekeeping job, I took my bike and rode down the street, feeling very happy about my decision to buy the bike. I glided smoothly downhill, but suddenly, as the ground leveled, something happened to the gears on the bike and it wouldn't go no matter how hard I pedaled. Disappointed that my new wheels had broken down so soon, I pushed it to a gas station where I left it and walked the rest of the way. I dreaded being late on my first day.

My lady employer was not at all impressed, and continued to yell even when I tried to explain what had happened. She was late for a meeting, and instead of taking time to listen to my reason for being late, she cut me short by handing me a list of the chores she expected me to perform and the order in which she wanted them done. Dust all the floors of the five-bedroom house, vacuum all the carpeted rooms, make the beds, change the bed sheets, iron the basketful of clothes, clean the walls, the cooker, the fridge, mop the floor, dust all the furniture, wash all the glasses and put the dishes away.

By five o'clock that evening, I was so tired I could hardly stand up straight. When the woman of the house came back, she went around the house inspecting my work before paying me. She was pleased with the work, and told me I could continue and come back to work the following week.

On my way home, I passed by the gas station where I picked up my bicycle and pushed it home. The following day, I went back to the bicycle dealer and told him that the bike he'd sold to me was faulty.

On hearing this, he became extremely arrogant and defensive, saying that he could not refund any money but that I could add more money on top of the 25 dollars I had already paid and exchange that bike for a new one. I reluctantly paid him for a new bicycle and left feeling taken advantage of.

Once again, I found myself at the receiving end of America's ruthless man-eat-man culture. The more I tried to wrap my head around this cruelty, the stranger and more inhumane it seemed to be.

Growing up as children in the village, we were led to believe that white people were very honest and sincere in all their dealings. However, here I was being taken advantage of by a white man. I felt conned and very bitter, especially after he told me that it was my fault because I didn't check to see if the bicycle was in good condition. It was then that I began to realize that my belief about the nature of white people was false.

I remembered Florence and her 17-year-old son arguing with each other, using extremely nasty language and she would say how she could not wait for him to move out. It was unheard of to talk back to your elders where I came from, let alone be so disrespectful as to hurl insults at them. Yet again, I found myself at crossroads between what I had been taught growing up in the village, and what the world was actually like. Everyone here seemed to be out for their own gain and never hesitated to step on their fellow citizens to achieve their desires. The contrast between my African beliefs and the reality of American life baffled me. It seemed to me that I was extremely naïve, holding on to my African norms and values which just did not apply to this new American world.

For example, in America, it was normal and acceptable for women to go out to parties, to drink alcohol, and to smoke. I recall one time a friend once invited me over to her mother's house for dinner. As we pulled up to the driveway, she warned me to ignore any bad behavior or disrespect her mother may show in my presence. Her mother was an alcoholic and therefore constantly drunk, and sure enough, as soon as we stepped into the house, we found her lying on the sofa passed out from heavy drinking throughout the day. This all seemed very strange to me as I had never seen a woman drink alcohol, let alone getting drunk.

As the housekeeping jobs were too physically demanding for me, I decided to try out babysitting. At my first babysitting job interview, the woman of the house was a condescending woman who made me feel inferior because of my African origin.

I tried my best to persevere at the babysitting job, but unfortunately, it didn't work out because it was very difficult to communicate with her child who could not understand what I was saying due to my African accent. The job was also very demanding as I had to spend a lot of time with the child, taking him to swimming lessons and walks to the park as well as any other activity that his mother saw fit.

Exasperated and overwhelmed, I made up my mind to go knocking from door to door around the neighborhood asking if anyone needed any help. On the third door that I knocked on, a middle-aged white woman answered. After I had explained to her that I was looking for work, she agreed to take me in but on a trial basis. I took instructions on the domestic chores I was to attend to, which were more like my first housekeeping job.

At around midday, the lady invited me to rest a little and have a sandwich which she had made. Even though I was starving, I politely declined her offer because I had been watching her as she walked her dog around the compound, patting it and carrying it around all morning while I was busy cleaning the house. I could not bear the thought of eating a sandwich that had been made with her unwashed hands.

At the end of the day, I was tired and worn out, but the pay was good and the lady asked me to come back every other day. I was soon able to save enough money to pay my tuition fees and used the extra money to buy my first car, a used blue Buick.

STRUGGLING TO MAKE THE AMERICAN DOLLAR

When the new semester began, I decided to get a job as a waitress in a restaurant that was close to campus. It was run by an old Jewish man, his wife, and their son. I was required to report to work in a white uniform and a white cap. I had to learn and memorize the names of the different dishes and drinks on the menu, many of which had French and Italian names.

During my first few days working there, I often carried the menu home so that my friend could help me memorize the names of the dishes and drinks that were especially difficult to pronounce. In order to help me understand what a customer had ordered, I learned to associate names on the menu with familiar words that I knew like *Bloody Mary, Tom Collins, Negroni, Maiden's Frayer* and *Screwdriver.*

Customers usually had drinks with their meals and they would ask what was available. I usually pronounced some of the drinks incorrectly, and thankfully, many of my customers upon realizing that I was an apprentice would try to be as helpful as possible.

When this happened, the head waitress would give me a cold penetrating stare that she never gave to other waitresses who were white and well versed with the routine. I could tell she didn't like me at all. Luckily, I made friends with one waitress at the restaurant who also attended the same college with me and who was of great assistance in helping me get acquainted with the work.

I would report to work at exactly 3 PM every day after class and I would leave by 9 PM. However, even with my friend helping me, I found the work too hard and every day seemed like it would be my last. I recall one evening I was so exhausted that I dropped a whole tray of food. The Head Waitress called me into the kitchen and screamed at me, asking me if I was crazy. Sometimes I would experience customers who would sneak away without paying after eating, or I would get the wrong order and the customer would decline to take the meal. In such cases, the money was deducted from my pay. Difficult as this was for me, I tried my best to do well and prayed that I wouldn't get fired.

With my classes and busy work schedule, my social life was nonexistent. When I was not working, I would be studying or too tired to do anything after being on my feet for most of the day. In my third year, I couldn't take the strain and loneliness anymore, and I decided that I would only take up full-time employment during the summer holiday and work part-time during school time. That year, the school's work placement office got me a job at a food processing factory, which prepared and packaged Mexican food.

The dress code was jeans and waterproof shoes. My shift began at 3 p.m. after my classes and ended at 9 p.m. On my first day, the supervisor took me out to the assembly line and I was placed a few feet from a huge machine that mixed flour and water and churned it out into little balls of dough. These were rolled down a conveyor belt to another section, where workers were lined up on both sides.

The balls were flattened and a meat mixture poured inside. The dough-meat combination was then folded into a neat piece and then baked before being packed into boxes. Everybody had to work very fast and the supervisor was moving from one spot to the other, ensuring that the work got done as efficiently as possible.

There was only one break from the endless standing inside the factory, and after a few months, my back was killing me and I could not carry on much longer. I discovered that most of the people working at the factory were not college students themselves which made it easier for them to keep up with their hectic schedules; while for me, I had to persevere through manual work on top of the stress of my academics.

Financial constraints and academic demands weighed heavily on me. I had left the family I was staying with and I was renting a room from a difficult old lady I could hardly get along with, who insisted on approving all my visitors and had a curfew imposed on me. The physical demands of the work at the Mexican food factory proved too much for me and consequently I left the company for a job at a computer chip manufacturer.

The work at the manufacturing plant was less physically demanding because all I was required to do was sit on a chair and watch for any anomalies and defects on the chips under a microscope lens. I took up the 11 p.m. to 7 a.m. shift, which I found convenient.

In the beginning, the job did not appear to be difficult, however, I soon found it hard to stay awake at work because I failed to get enough sleep. I was only supposed to keep one eye closed at the microscope, but sometimes my boss would find me half asleep with both eyes closed.

I learned that many of the workers used to sneak into the toilet to catch some winks for a few minutes, so while other people went to smoke during their breaks, I would go to the toilet to catch a quick nap. Eventually, I started to lose my voice and my eyes had a permanent blood-shot look to them from sleep deprivation. The mental and physical strain was too much for me to bear and after only six months, I found myself looking for yet another job opening.

From the time I landed in the United States, I had only lived and worked in white neighborhoods. However, I genuinely longed to meet and interact with Black Americans. I was intrigued by the fact that we shared a common origin and anxiously waited for an opportunity to get to know them and understand their culture.

I had seen some Black Americans in campus, but I had not had the chance to get to know them outside of the classroom. One evening, as I was walking out of campus, I saw a black girl, who I shared a class with, standing all by herself. She seemed friendly, so I decided to approach her and introduce myself.

I asked her if she was an African student and she smiled warmly at me and told me she was African American. After the introductions, she excitedly asked me to go with her and meet some other Black Americans who were seated nearby. When we joined them, she announced, "Hey meet this sister from Africa, she is One-n-ziko." My name was clearly too hard for her to pronounce properly.

One of the boys in the group sprang to his feet and told me how welcome I was to their group. I felt such warmth at being received this way and I immediately concluded in my mind that my first few months in America would not have been so lonely had I met them earlier.

Another boy asked me to tell them about Africa and all about the culture and lifestyle. Excitement broke out all over their faces as they began to ask some of the most ignorant and stupid questions I ever heard. One of them even asked me if there were any houses in Africa, and everyone broke out laughing. Another one asked if people wore clothes as the laughter got even louder. I felt so offended and thought they were the most ignorant and impolite people I had ever met. I was tempted to walk away, but instead, I faced them squarely and boldly told them that even although Africa was not as developed as America was, it still had big cities and five-star hotels. I told them that Africa was a continent and not a country as some Americans ignorantly thought, and they should probably have asked me about my country, Kenya. Immediately, their laughter died down, and one of them apologized for being so insensitive.

Whenever I got the chance, I always tried to mingle with black people, and as time went by, I was able to make a few black friends on campus and even got to know their families. I liked how they talked, and

I began to use phrases like, "He is a bad Joe" or "We got wasted" or "She is crazy" in an attempt to try and fit in. I also learned that there were many African students in my college and other surrounding colleges who I could visit and, to my surprise, I came to find out that some were from my homeland, Kenya.

The feelings that rushed through me on meeting Kenyans in the United States could only be described as heavenly. My heart leaped and screamed with joy. Suddenly, I wasn't so lonely anymore. I felt a heavy burden lift from my shoulders as the world began to make sense and I began to see life in color again. It seemed as though I had waited all my life for this moment. A sense of assurance took root within me. I knew that from here on, my life was going to get easier and that brighter days had begun.

1. At the at University   2. In My room at the Krafts   3. At a University Summer Party Dancing
4. In my room at Florence's House during Summer   5. During my stay with the Krafts

1. Me Third from Left, with some Friends Going Out for a Meal
2. With a Friend in California
3. With my American Boyfriend
4. With my Brother Evans and his children Mukuria, Nyambura and Githae. Leaving hospital in California with his new baby

LOVE, HEARTBREAK AND
A YOUTHFUL LIFE

"Nothing ever goes away until it teaches us what we need to know."
— Pema Chodron

When I was in high school in Kenya, there was a popular magazine publication called *Drum* that many girls at my school loved to read. The magazine's popularity was mainly due to the fact that it contained a pen pal section where people would send in their personal profiles, seeking pen pals from all over the world. My friends would excitedly read through the different profiles of people seeking friends and would write to the ones that they liked most.

Sometimes, these exchanges would turn into serious relationships. I remember one girl who met a young doctor from Zambia in this way. After she finished school, he actually came to meet her and her family, and they ended up happily married.

For some reason, I just wasn't excited about pen pals and communicating with people in far off lands who I could not meet or see with my own eyes. My first relationship, which was totally unexpected, blossomed when I was in form three. I had attended a high school dance when a boy approached me and started a conversation. I remember thinking that he was the most handsome boy I had ever laid eyes on. Mugo was his name, and he was one year ahead of me at school.

He was very shy and almost never talked to girls, although all the girls at school admired him. To my surprise, and to the envy of my friends, he walked up to me and asked if I would dance with him. I was very excited and although I was shy, I couldn't say no.

Mugo was a quiet, shy person from a wealthy family. His father owned a construction company and because of this, they were well known and respected in the community. Their house was made of iron sheets, with a foundation that was lifted two feet off the ground, which was a big deal back then. It was fitted with glass windows, and its walls were painted green, while the roof was a screaming red. To me, this was the ideal house. His family had two cars and many servants working for them.

After the night of the dance, he began coming over regularly to my parents' house to see me. Since he feared my parents, he would bring his sister along with him in the pretense that she was the one who wanted to see me. At other times, he would send my cousin to get me as he waited by the gate. I would go out to meet him, and we would chat away for hours. It was more of a cat and mouse game, and I enjoyed the sneaking around immensely.

After we had gotten to know each other rather well, he asked me out on a date, which I found myself immediately agreeing to. He picked me up in his father's vehicle and we sped off towards Kenyatta University where we were supposed to attend a dance. His father was a professor at the university, and he had invited Mugo to the dance with his friends.

I wore a pink, sleeveless dress, very high heeled shoes that I could barely walk in and some of my hand-me-down stockings which I would get from my cousin Lucy. Many times, the stockings would have holes in them and to cover them up I would put on two pairs of stockings at the same time so the areas that were torn in one pair could be covered by the other.

We arrived at Kenyatta University to find a lively crowd and good music, but because I was very shy, I spent the whole time seated at my table, watching others having a good time. I mostly had my eye on my date, who walked around socializing with a beer bottle in one hand and a cigarette in the other because it was cool to be seen smoking and drinking in those days.

Although my siblings and I had secretly indulged in alcohol on several occasions at parties and ceremonies, I did not drink that night as I didn't want to embarrass myself in front of him. Later that night, after he dropped me home, I remember feeling excited at the thought that I now had a boyfriend who could take me places, even if it was only in his father's truck.

The first time I tasted alcohol was at one of my cousin's pre-wedding party in Kenya. He was a very learned man who had just landed a very good job with the government. Since it was a formal dinner and very respectable people had been invited, children were not allowed to attend. However, being the naughty children that we were, we decided to crash the party.

At some point during the event, my friend offered me a sweet drink, which tasted like spicy porridge. A few sips in, I began to feel a little light headed. I ended up taking several cups of the sweet, spicy sips, not knowing that the drink was actually a local alcoholic brew made from maize meal.

Shortly afterward, I was completely drunk and unable to walk or see straight. I don't even remember how I got home although I do remember my furious mother yelling at me because I arrived home so late. I was lucky because she didn't realize I was drunk. Otherwise, she would have skinned me alive.

Back home, if anyone asked you out on a date, it was taken as an obvious sign that they wanted to sleep with you. In the United States, however, things were completely different. When a boy asked you out on a date, it actually meant that they wanted to take you out for a movie or lunch and nothing more. Growing up, our elders had trained us to believe that any relationship or contact with a man would always be about sex.

While I was still new to American culture, someone told me that Sexually-Transmitted Infections (STIs) were so common there that people referred to them as colds. I learned that compared to our African culture, it was more accepted for men to be gay.

I learned that in certain areas and across a certain demographic, it was considered cool to smoke pot and pose for nudist magazines. Many people carried guns and shootings were numerous. All in all, the definition of freedom and liberty in America was all too strange and bizarre to me.

As I settled into this strange new culture, I began to realize that almost everyone, both old and young, was in some sort of relationship that didn't necessarily entail marriage. I would always see couples doing different things together such as mountain climbing, going to the beach or to the movies.

Friday nights were considered date nights. It was almost a strange thing to be single in America, and it did not take long before I felt the need to find someone to be with.

A few years into my stay in the United States, I began dating an American boy who I shared classes with. He was tall with short curly hair and I remember him being very masculine. He had a brilliant mind and was also very creative. But the thing I loved about him most was that he was very committed to me.

Back home, it was taboo to marry a white man. African women who chose to date or marry white men were frowned upon and disrespected by their fellow Africans as well as their communities. For these reasons, African women who chose to date white men distanced themselves from their kin in order to avoid criticism.

My white boyfriend was quite curious about life in Africa and sometimes he would even talk about settling in Kenya with me. He would come with me to our Kenyan parties and showed a genuine interest in learning African languages although he would quickly become upset when the African men spoke in their mother tongues when he was around, almost as if to show him that he was not welcome there. The Kenyan men felt that he was overstepping his boundaries by dating me.

My white boyfriend was a good man, but he was very hot-tempered. Whenever he became angry about something, he would shake uncontrollably as he spoke. His hot temper made him do some very irrational things.

One time, he was trying to convert me into a Seventh-day Adventist and one Saturday, after he had dragged me to church with him, he asked me whether I had enjoyed the service. I carelessly responded that I didn't know if I enjoyed it because I hadn't paid much attention anyway. He got so angry that he slapped me hard for my indifferent attitude towards his religion. I remember being so upset and did not speak to him for some time, choosing to avoid him as I seriously contemplated if our relationship would work.

As time went by, he became aware that he had anger issues and began to work on controlling himself better. Our relationship blossomed, and we fell so deeply in love that he even introduced me to his parents and eventually proposed to me. I excitedly wrote home, telling them the good news and seeking my parents' blessing. But to my surprise, my father wrote back a resounding no to my intentions to get married to a white man. I was heartbroken.

He had come into my life at a time when I was struggling to fit into life in America, and he helped me to adjust replacing my loneliness with companionship and friendship. I felt very secure with him in my life, and the thought of leaving him made me sick. Despite my feelings for my boyfriend, I chose to obey my father's instruction and ended the relationship.

After I had left him, in blind obedience to my parents, I fell into isolation once more, and my loneliness only got worse. I was going through my heartbreak alone with no one in the world to share in my pain. My American boyfriend wondered why I suddenly gave him the cold shoulder, and did everything he could to try and reconcile with me.

Despite my longing for him, I was more afraid of being a disgrace in the eyes of my family and bringing shame to them. However, deep down I felt that this was unfair and that there was more to life than fulfilling other's expectations. I wondered if I would even fit in when I eventually went back home because I had been almost completely de-cultured by my stay in the United States. Despite this blow to my relationship and after much soul-searching, I resolved to move on.

Later on, in my third and final year of my undergraduate studies, I met another man at a foreign students' party. He was Nigerian, studying for his post-graduate degree and he was also the editor of the school magazine. He was eloquent and handsome; most of the girls liked him although I was not initially attracted to him because I knew that he had a girlfriend. As time went by, his girlfriend finished her studies and returned back to her motherland-Nigeria. A few months after she left, we got closer, and we began going out.

When I met the Nigerian, I thought that because he was black, we would understand each other better as we were both from African cultures. However, this was not the reality. Our cultures were worlds apart and sometimes I felt that I got along better with white people than I did with my Nigerian boyfriend. After dating for only a month, he wanted a serious relationship. He began talking about the future and things we would do after we finished our education, including moving with him back to Nigeria.

Feeling a bit ambushed and pressured, I told him that my parents were a huge part of my life, and any decision I made would require their approval. I also told him that my parents required me to finish my education before I started thinking about marriage. He however stubbornly insisted that he wanted to marry me immediately and whisk me off to Nigeria after our studies.

I, therefore, felt compelled to lie to him that I had another boyfriend back home who would write me letters regularly since we were still in a relationship. He had no idea that the letters were actually from my former boyfriend back home who was simply writing to check in on me. Even though I had ended that relationship before traveling to America, he immediately asked for the address and wrote a letter to my 'Kenyan boyfriend' terminating our long-distance relationship and informing him that I was now in a serious relationship. He also wrote a letter to introduce himself to my parents which I was pressured into sending.

The man was very domineering, and even today I can't understand why I let him have so much control over me. Although he seemed very fond of me, he had a controlling attitude which made me uncomfortable.

One time he asked me to sell a very beautiful car that I had bought for myself so that we could send the money back to Nigeria, as he said we needed to start preparing for our future back in his home country. Other times he would complain about how I was dressed when he picked me up for dates, and would even make me change my attire before we left. He would often criticize me and this had a very damaging effect on my self-esteem.

After a while, he wrote another letter to my parents talking about our plans to be together and to move to Nigeria. My father's response to his requests was, again, a resounding no. My father didn't want to hear any of that 'nonsense' as he called it. He had a negative attitude towards West African men and in a separate letter personally addressed to me, he proceeded to remind me of my cousin who married a Ghanaian man against her family's wishes. She had a good career as a doctor, but a few years down the line, she went completely insane, and it was believed that the man had driven her to this state. I was strongly warned to stay away from West African men lest the same fate befell me.

After yet another sour rebuttal from my own parents, I again relapsed into a fit of strain and depression as the words from my father's letter haunted me. As if on cue, a letter from my mother followed soon after my father's containing the same warning, but sterner and with a promise of dire consequences if I disobeyed both my parents.

Once again, I found myself in a dilemma because I thought my parents would be more accepting of my African boyfriend. I went through another period of loneliness, choosing to keep my tribulations bottled up. I longed to live like American girls of my age and to experience normal feelings of love. However, there was my upbringing, culture as well as expectations from society and family to contend with. I was torn between two worlds.

After two failed attempts at love, I decided to forget about relationships and buried myself in my books. Soon enough, the year was over, and I was finally due to graduate.

GRADUATION AND THE BIRTH OF MY SON

Graduation day found me homesick with memories of mom, dad, and friends I would have loved to invite to the occasion. I was sad that there would be no crowd cheering me on in my proudest moment and present to witness the toil of my life rewarded.

I hired a photographer to capture every detail of the occasion so that I could send the pictures to my family, who were far away in Cura village. I imagined my mother probably working on the farm at that time, totally oblivious of how much I longed to see her again. There would be no replacement for the void I felt without them.

My only consolation was the gown that frocked me in triumph and achievement, and the tassel that brushed away at my eyes and reminded me that I had made it to the helm of academic credit. It was a bittersweet day for African students like me.

Graduation was a nostalgic occasion for many students, as it also marked the end of one chapter in their lives and the beginning of another. They walked into the graduation square filled with emotion and dreams, and so many other desires that they had now drawn even closer to accomplishing. Some said they wanted to get married and have children, while others wanted to go on with their post-graduate studies. Still, others wanted to work for a few years before going back to school.

For me, there were two choices before me. I could either continue with my postgraduate studies or fly back to Kenya to find a job. Even before I completed my undergraduate degree, I had already decided that I would further my education in the United States. Prior to my finishing school, I applied to several institutions for a place in a Master's Degree program. My graduation found me waiting for a response from the various colleges.

A few weeks after graduation, I received a letter of admission into a postgraduate course at Assumption College, which is a Catholic college based in Massachusetts. I applied to colleges in Massachusetts because I had met a young man from my village back home who was now living in Boston.

He was a childhood acquaintance from Cura and was well known to my family. We had grown fond of each other over time, and I was keen to know him better. My cousin, who was good friends with him, had mentioned that I was also in the United States, and therefore he sought me out.

We got to know each other over many phone calls and visits, and I came to realize that he was a good guy and had all the qualities that I desired in a husband. He often told me how much he missed his family and how he longed to go back home so that he could be there for his mother. He was also hard working and was always putting his money in wise investments. In short, we had similar goals in life.

I began preparing to leave for my new school right away. It was a sad affair saying goodbye to all my friends in California, friends I had lived with, cried with, danced with, and shared treasured moments with; friends who had helped me cope with the indifference of a society so unlike my own.

After I moved to Massachusetts to begin pursuing my master's degree, we became even closer, and soon afterward, we decided to take the bold step and introduce each other to our families. I prayed that this time, my parents would say yes to our plans to get married. To my great joy, there were more accepting to this relationship than my previous relationships. Immediately we started planning our wedding.

Meanwhile, after moving from California to Massachusetts, it became quite expensive to keep in touch with Mr. and Mrs. Kraft. We would therefore only speak on phone once a month, at which point I would update them on everything that was going on in my new University. I was anxious as well as excited to invite them to my wedding but unfortunately at the time they were not able to travel to the East Coast to join me on my big day.

The wedding took place at a small church, with about one hundred people in attendance. Although some of my friends believed that we had rushed into marriage too quickly, we were both sick of being lonely and felt ready to settle into a meaningful life. Like me, he had a strong desire to fulfill his mother's wishes by marrying a girl from his home and community.

A few months later, during the winter season, we had a baby boy. I was just two weeks away from graduating with my Master's Degree when the baby came, a bouncing baby boy, who we named Kironyo.

I was extremely excited to be a mother. I read everything I could lay my hands on about bringing up and caring for a baby. However, as a new mother, I was very anxious. I spent most of my days wondering whether my baby was safe and comfortable, whether I was over feeding him, or whether he was warm enough.

My anxiety only grew worse as I fed myself with all kinds of literature on baby care. I even made a wooden board, according to the instruction from a baby care magazine, against which the baby would be held, lest someone hold him the wrong way and strain his neck and back. Unknown to me, my cautious ways only left my baby more vulnerable. In his early years, Kironyo was frail and thin, as I was too cautious when feeding him and too protective of him to simply let him grow.

The birth of our son and the fact that I wasn't well enough to work meant that our finances were strained. Since I was at home with the baby, my husband had to work around the clock to feed and maintain his young family.

It did not help that Kironyo was born during what was recorded as the coldest winter in Massachusetts in the last 20 years and the thought of getting out of the house even for fresh air was considered absurd, particularly for a newborn baby. I began to get emotionally and physically frustrated.

Six weeks after I gave birth, I was well enough to work and therefore I found a job to help my husband keep up with the rent, maintain our two cars as well as to pay for my school fees and student loans.

The winter was severe and our daily attire included heavy coats and warm clothing. Constantly digging the car out of the snow made me very homesick as I terribly missed the sun and my family even more.

After I had finished college, my husband and I began making plans to fly back home, and we began putting some money aside towards the financing of the trip. Eventually, we had enough to start a new life back home, and it was time to leave the United States. Although we had much to look forward to, the prospect of leaving America, probably for good, made me feel melancholic and uncertain about beginning a new life for our new family.

As the day of our departure approached, I felt very sad about leaving America after having lived there for seven years. I had spent all my adult life in the country, having made it through without depending on my real family.

In the course of my postgraduate studies, I often thought long and hard about how my life would have been if it were not for my chance encounter with the Krafts. I thought about the enormous educational and cultural influences America had on me. I wondered whether I would be able to reconcile these influences with the expectations of my family and society when I returned to Kenya.

For seven years, I struggled and finally lived and adapted to a foreign way of life, quite different from the way I had been brought up. I imagined that going back home would be like going back to a lost dream and time. However, the urge to go back home was too strong; I longed to see my family and to introduce my new family to them.

GOING BACK TO MY ROOTS: KARIBU KENYA

"Sometimes we have to leave home in order to find out what we left there, and why it matters so much". – Shauna Niequist

After seven eventful years that seemed like an eternity, the day I had been longing for during my entire stay in the United States had come. I was finally going back home to my motherland and my people.

My husband, my son, and I boarded the London-bound flight at 0900hrs, and we were in the air shortly afterward. On the plane, thoughts about the life I was leaving behind filled my mind. Departure was a teary affair for me. I wasn't sure if it was because of the presence of our many friends, who had come to say their goodbyes or the reality that I was leaving my second life and my home away from home, not knowing if I would ever return again.

My husband and I had sent lots of luggage ahead by ship while we took the rest with us on the plane. Once we got to London, we were in transit for about two hours before boarding another flight to Kenya.

I remember feeling as if I was in a dream. I had thought about this moment for seven years of my life, and the fact that I was actually living my dream seemed too good to be true. Reality finally sunk in when the stewardess announced that we were now entering Kenyan airspace; the scenery of Lake Turkana and Lake Nakuru became distinctly visible as the plane began its slow descent.

Nothing in the world can compare to a Kenyan landscape from the air; filled with splendor and color. The Rift Valley looks like a long table cloth, decorated with shimmering silver lakes and green rolling hills. Its valleys are covered in lush vegetation, and a sublime landscape dotted with trees, flowers, and unforgettable beauty.

We soon landed in Nairobi and spent about half an hour clearing with the Customs Department. I will never forget those first precious moments as I emerged from the plane and walked on Kenyan ground for what seemed like the very first time in my life. A wide grin was plastered on my face, and my eyes were unable to focus on any one thing as they darted from place to place. The airport looked exactly the same; the people just as lost and confused as they bid their traveling loved ones' goodbye, while others waited for their people to touch down.

As we waited for our luggage to emerge at the automated luggage deck, I suddenly spotted my parents some distance away. I recognized them immediately despite the years since I last saw them, and I couldn't help but fly towards them, almost dropping poor Kironyo in the process. When they saw me running towards them, their expressions transformed into wide smiles as they too surged towards me.

The feelings and emotions coursing through me in that moment were simply divine. As I joyfully embraced my parents, my husband approached us, and I finally got the chance to introduce my new family to my mom and dad. Surprisingly, my Kikuyu was still as flawless as it had been seven years ago, and my parents, though slightly aged, had not changed much at all.

After the introductions and a little conversation, we walked outside to find a huge crowd of village folk waiting. The sight of the crowd brought back memories of my departure, which now seemed like a lifetime ago. The crowd met us with song and dance, welcoming us back home and thanking the Almighty for delivering me back to them safe and sound. We sang and danced all the way to the parking lot where vehicles were waiting to ferry us home.

"Home is where you can always return no matter how long you have been gone"

Driving through Nairobi was a shock; the city had really changed during my absence. It seemed to have stretched and extended in all directions. I was also shocked to see people on the streets who still looked distressed and after all these years still seemed to be struggling to survive. There were many people on the streets, walking in all directions and milling around at bus stops. In the United States, people were mainly in their cars and rarely walked across town.

As we pulled into the local village shopping centre, I was surprised to see scores of men standing outside the shops gazing into nothing. In contrast, the women were busy selling their farm produce in makeshift stalls with babies so tightly strapped to their backs that they couldn't fall off even if the women bent over to pick something up.

I wondered how it was possible that a woman could walk barefoot in this day and age while carrying heavy loads in homemade sisal baskets on her back. As our entourage snaked its way through the village, people stopped to gaze at the passing vehicles. It felt like time had stood still since I left. Not much had changed here.

To my surprise, we arrived home to find an even larger crowd of villagers who were not able to come to the airport. My husband and I were accosted with a barrage of questions about the strange land we had come from. The questions sounded as absurd to me as the tales we narrated sounded to them. Some asked if there was soil on the ground. Others wanted to know what kind of food people ate in America. Some people began to gossip saying that I had forgotten how to speak my mother tongue. I felt cornered and besieged.

After I had come back to Kenya, I was at pains to explain to the villagers why I had not amassed any wealth while in America and why I had not been able to change my family's financial outlook. Back in the 70s, if you were fortunate enough to travel to the United States and find a job there, you were thought of as the 'savior' of your people back home. As soon as you started earning, your family expected you to send them money for their upkeep as well as anything else they required.

Africans living in the United States found themselves making enormous sacrifices in order to meet these huge expectations of their folks back home. They did their best to give the impression that they were very successful and accomplished, but the reality was much different. Many of these people were often juggling two or three jobs at the same time and some eventually chose to completely disconnect themselves from the people back home so as to escape this massive pressure.

Now that I was home, I began to feel the pressure to get a job and start earning an income. Therefore, a mere two days after our arrival, I seriously began searching for a job. My husband and I found an apartment through a newspaper advert, but the rent was a whopping four thousand shillings a month. I wondered how much money one had to earn so as to afford bare necessities like rent, water, power, and a telephone.

Life here seemed very expensive compared to America. As we tried to manage the enormous expenses, I also realized that people's expectations of me had now completely changed. Neighbors and supposed friends would walk into the apartment at any time claiming to be visiting and instead end up asking me to give them things like clothes or items that I had brought back with me from the United States. I realized that the people had a sense of entitlement, as if what was mine also belonged to them.

Another thing that irked me was the fact that there were no developed towns or shopping centers in remote areas like my village. A task as simple as buying groceries entailed traversing the whole area, moving from shop to shop until you got everything you needed. If you wanted a supermarket, you had to go into the city.

One morning, I woke up bright and early and prepared for another long day of job hunting. As I was waiting at the bus stop for a ride into town, I was shocked to see a passenger service vehicle, or *matatu* as they were called, filled to the brim and overflowing with excess passengers. Some couldn't even fit inside the small van, and they were hanging dangerously at the door, holding on to whatever they could to keep from falling off. I soon learnt that it was normal for *'matatus'* to carry excess passengers and behave recklessly on the roads.

A bus that had some empty seats finally pulled up and I got in. As we drove along the Uhuru highway, I saw workers from the Kibera slum walking to their places of work in the city center and further downtown in the industrial area. They could not afford to pay so they had to walk a long distance to get to town.

It began to dawn on me that Kenya was an impoverished country whose brilliant beginning had all but backfired. The people had been left to fend for themselves while those in higher offices filled their coffers. I became sad and bitter every time I thought about the Mau Mau and other political heroes who struggled to liberate our nation. It seemed all their efforts had been in vain.

When I got to town, I headed straight to the office of a certain director of a firm in the city. When I arrived, his secretary informed me that he was not in and that she did not have any idea when he would be back. I waited till 10 a.m. before my patience grew thin and I instead decided to leave a message with his secretary.

As I continued my search for a stable job, I realized that people in Nairobi seemed to rely more on informal canvassing and personal introductions to secure jobs rather than using a formal procedure or their academic qualifications. I also learned that keeping time and appointments was not taken as seriously in Kenya as it was in the United States. I learned not to be in a hurry when having meetings with people because conversations seemed to go on forever.

I realized that I was still the same girl, who had been plucked from village life, yet I had somewhat changed. It was all very confusing. I wanted to help the people around me; I wanted to change my community; I wanted to meet their expectations: yet the situation was beyond my means and control. At best, I felt like a phony.

After I was done with my appointments for the day, I made my way to the bus stop so as to catch a bus back home. As I walked through the streets, I saw a crowd of irate youths chasing a pickpocket as they shouted "Thief! Thief!"

The pickpocket had apparently made away with a tourist's bag, leaving her there confused and in tears. I did not bother to stop as I was in a rush to relieve my husband, who was taking care of the baby while I was away. Still, this event lingered in my mind, and I couldn't help but wonder if Kenya had really developed or regressed in my years away.

A few weeks after we jetted in, my mother helped us find a babysitter to help me look after the baby as well as carry out general house chores like cooking and cleaning. The girl was eager to work and told me that she had once been employed in Kilimani, and was experienced in-house work and child care. She told me a touching story of how she had dropped out of secondary school in form two due to lack of school fees.

Although I wondered whether to trust this stranger with my child, I recalled my early years back in America, trying to survive through odd jobs and I felt compelled to give her a chance. I also took on the responsibility and paid for her to attend a secretarial college. At the end of the first month, after I had paid her wages, she politely asked for some time off so that she could take some of the money home to her parents. Of course, I consented to her request, thinking to myself that she was a very responsible young woman.

Early the next morning as she was getting ready to leave, I discovered that some of my clothes and even my sons were missing. On looking through her bag, I discovered the clothes neatly folded. I couldn't believe it. After all I had done to help her, I felt betrayed that she would try to steal from me.

The following week, I went to see my family back in the village. Even there, people came up to me with strange requests. Some wanted me to get jobs for their children in the city while some of my cousins wanted to move into my house and stay with my husband and I while they looked for jobs.

This presented me with a dilemma: Here I was struggling to settle down and try to get a proper job myself, but on the other hand, here were these people convinced that because of my education I had the power to solve all their woes.

One time, an old man from the village saw me in a *matatu* and remarked, "Why do these educated people from overseas use public means of the transportation like the rest of us?" I could immediately feel the community's great expectations for individuals like myself.

It took me about a month to land my first job in Kenya and almost a year after that before I was able to afford a car. My husband and I bought a used vehicle for the price of what a new car would cost in the United States. I was bewildered and wondered how people managed to survive in Kenya with such high standards of living.

Our jobs did not provide us with much money and for the first few months, we literally lived from hand to mouth, using all we earned on food and basic necessities. We could do very little to help our parents and siblings financially. I thought of how hard I struggled to acquire my education only to come back home and feel totally lost and uprooted from the culture and people that I had known. I was geographically in Kenya, but psychologically in America.

My home, Kenya, seemed like a very strange and unfamiliar place. I wondered about the girls I'd grown up with. I missed them now more than ever, but in what was now a strange place, I would walk from one street to the next without coming across a single familiar face.

One day, I stopped for lunch at the Hilton Hotel in the heart of Nairobi city. I was surprised to find the place packed with white people and apart from the waiters, I was the only black person there. I ordered a plate of fries and a hamburger and remember feeling very much like I shouldn't have been there in the first place.

I kept wondering to myself whether I would ever fit in and feel at home in Kenya. I was stuck at a crossroad; sandwiched between two conflicting cultures. My people treated me like I was one of them, but regarded me as being from a different time and place. On the other hand, the Western world perceived me as inferior because of the color of my skin. Even in the capital city of my own motherland, I still felt like an outsider, and only names of familiar streets made me feel at home.

After a while, I came to discover that I was not alone. There were many people suffering a similar dilemma. Many of us had been uprooted from our rural communities and shipped off into a foreign land for further study. On coming back home, we were no longer able to fit back into the gaps we had left in our societies.

Nothing in Kenya felt genuine to me. There was nothing in Nairobi that gave me a truly African feel, apart from the stereotypical Maasai and Kamba soapstone crafts that were sold in shops. Nothing truly revealed to me what Kenya was really about.

I saw many people in my position, striving to recreate the lives they used to live while they were abroad by joining exclusive clubs and shunning community-based societies. I visited people who had lived in Kenya all their lives, and I realized they were just as lost as I was. There was little understanding of one another.

All their children spoke of were the latest disco hits and movies like *Dallas, the Jefferson's* and *San Fernando Scene*. Everything that was on TV, as well as Western pop music on the radio, made me feel as though I was back in the States, far away from Kenya.

I also observed the bias in the school system, much like the class and race system I'd witnessed in Boston and Los Angeles. The elite in Kenya sent their children to expensive schools that the rest of the people could only dream of. In Boston, the buses were segregated by one's color. There were buses for whites and buses for blacks. In Kenya, however, this hideous culture of segregation changed its creed from segregation by color to segregation by class and financial muscle. I felt lost and knew that it was up to me to take matters into my own hands if I was ever going to feel at home again.

1. Graduation Day 2. Graduation Day
3. With My Nigerian Boyfriend 4. With My Son Kironyo

1. With my Son Kironyo at our 1st House When we Moved Back from the US.
2. Mr. and Mrs. Kraft Visiting Kenya for the 1st Time and Meeting with my Parents Julius and Damaris Mukuria.
3. With My Daughter Wandia at 3 Months Old in Nairobi
4. Wandia and I in Nairobi
5. Being Interviewed as a Staff Member at the University of Nairobi
6. In a Meeting with the Women of Mathare Valley

LIFE IN THE SLUMS OF MATHARE VALLEY

"Being unwanted, unloved, uncared for and forgotten by everybody. I think that is a much greater hunger, a greater poverty than the person who has nothing to eat".
– Mother Teresa

After months of moving from one job to another trying to get a job that would sustain myself and my family, I was engaged as a young lecturer at the University of Nairobi. I was initially supposed to be teaching in the Psychology Department, but such a department did not exist at the time, and only one college in Kenya offered a Diploma in Social Work.

Psychology was an unpopular field, and I was yet to meet any other Kenyan scholar who had specialized in it. The university wanted me to work for them, but they were at a loss as to where to place me and so I began teaching in the Department of Sociology, which was the closest degree to Psychology.

After some time, several faculty members and I began to realize that there were many students who could be developed into social workers but were missing out on the opportunity because there was no social work degree in the country. Therefore, we decided to approach the university's vice chancellor with a proposal to start a degree program in social work.

This suggestion was warmly received, and soon the university began developing the courses needed for this degree program. Realizing that we also needed financial resources to set up the institution, we decided to approach the government and request for funding to start a social work department at the university. Fortunately, this request was also approved, and we were allowed, to begin with forty students annually.

I was assigned the role of the Program Coordinator, as well as given the task of identifying places where students could undertake field placements. At the time, Mama Ngina and Thomas Barnardo's children's homes were the only places that had a program where people could volunteer as social workers.

During my interactions with the staff and children in the homes, I came to learn about Mathare Valley and decided to visit the place so as to find out how we could incorporate it into our field activities in order to get more exposure for our students.

Back then, suburban Nairobi barely resembled today's upper-class estates like Lavington or Westlands. Slum dwellings were much larger and pronounced as compared to other housing estates. I wandered into Mathare Valley and saw a level of poverty that was appalling beyond comprehension.

What passed for houses were little huts that housed dozens of people. There was filth, litter, refuse and trenches of dark, diseased water, everywhere. There were no streets here; only narrow twists between huts. There were no toilets, and the strong stench of urine was everywhere with garbage piled recklessly into rotting heaps that had been there for months. A heavy, unmoving stench hung low in the air, emanating from the shallow, open trenches in which raw sewage flowed.

The weather on that day only made the situation worse. It was hot and humid, just before the rainy season was due to begin. Women were busy frying fish for sale on the sides of the narrow winding paths. Others lit charcoal jikos and kerosene stoves outside their little tin shacks. All these different pungency and smells fused together to give Mathare a 'unique' and disgusting stench that was unlike anything I had ever encountered before.

I remember covering my nose as I jumped over the blackened puddles and trenches of human waste. I was a stranger here, and it was obvious to the residents. The thing that moved me most about the whole experience was the people who lived in those shanties.

They looked shattered and resigned, hopeless and afraid, weary and bushed. Their children ran around in the muck, looking as grimy as the gutter in which they played their games. Drunken people staggered home looking haggard with bloodshot eyes and empty stares. Hopelessness hung in the air.

I had seen poverty as I grew up in the villages of Kabete and Cura, but nothing had prepared me for what I saw in Mathare Valley that unforgettable Friday afternoon. The sore sight that accosted my eyes was in my mind the effigy of degradation, a creation of treachery, and an act of felony against my fellow citizens.

I had spent seven years of my life abroad, studying in an American university, lived and interacted with some of the wealthiest people in the world and socialized with a culture and government that provided basic amenities like sanitation and food to its people. I had come to believe that it was a common principle to expect that for every community and more so for my own people.

Does the government know you live here? I almost asked aloud in disbelief. Feelings of anger and desperation raged uncontrollably within me. It was as though a dam had burst its banks and a flood of emotion had overcome me. I felt betrayed and utterly disillusioned by the menacing truth of the situation. My worldview and innocent albeit ignorant assumptions were challenged beyond measure by the conception of life in Mathare and the people living there.

My heart was filled with deep grief and despair for my countrymen. All my accomplishments suddenly seemed extraneous and insignificant. All the confidence and belief I had placed in society, as well as my conception of life as it should be all disintegrated in that one moment of deep consternation. I felt lonely and disheartened. Lost.

In the 80s, Mathare slum was bursting at the seams with close to two hundred thousand residents. Nairobi had become a city under duress from a burst in a population that was straining the town's resources far beyond its limits.

The city council was ill-equipped and struggling to provide housing, water, and sanitation for the rapidly increasing population. Most of the people coming into the town were poor and resorted to living on the outskirts, making up an endless clutter of slum dwellers living under the most squalid conditions.

The tin and cardboard shanties that held the people hostage made the ramshackle dwellings of the villager's upcountry look like paradise. These miserable cages were home to families as big as eight or more, mostly women and children. The people stayed out of the huts most of the day; the children playing, the adults drinking the illicit local brew popularly known as chang'aa, and women busy trying to find what little food they could find to prepare for the children.

There was little resemblance of civilization here, and the place was one ugly den characterized by a pungent odor. There was no electricity in Mathare, no schools or clinics, no sewerage or water drainage systems of any kind, and no paved roads—just dirt and litter.

The majority of the slum dwellers were women and children. Social change over the post-independence days had resulted in fatherless children and violated women who had no economic means.

Every single woman in the slum of Mathare seemed to have a history of domestic violence, family conflict or a child brought into the world under strain and stress. There were so many women falling pregnant, a lot of physical abuse and runaways who all ended up in Mathare slum.

The children didn't go to school and instead played in the neighborhood all day long. Those who were old enough helped their mothers in their small stalls, or they would collect scrap metal which they would sell for a few shillings.

People in Mathare would take advantage of any situation that they could; the population was growing and demand for housing as well as other basic necessities like water was extremely high. If you had a small room, you would subdivide it and sublet it to someone so as to earn an extra income. There would be illegally connected water and electricity for which cartels would charge a small fee.

The city council did not require the shop and stall owners to have a license to operate their businesses because it was too chaotic for the council officers to come around and demand to see a license. This attracted criminals and other opportunists to the slum and encouraged them to continue in their illegal ways in search of quick money without fear of being caught.

The men of Mathare Valley were broken job seekers who had sunk into acquiescence after facing the harsh realities of unemployment and lack of money. Most fell into alcohol abuse as life in the shanties tightened its grip on them. They were very aggressive because of the community and environment that they lived in. They would mostly be interested in the kind of jobs which required aggression like night watchmen, guards, and other security-related jobs.

One of the saddest things about Mathare was that the enormous, impoverished population were shamelessly exploited by politicians who merely used them to get votes. Due to the fact that most of the people were alcoholics, as little as 50 shillings was enough to get someone to vote for you.

If the politicians needed some hooligans to create chaos in another part of the country, they would stop a truck anywhere on the street, and the young men with nothing better to do would jump in without knowing where they were going. If they were required to carry out a demonstration, the men would accept a very small fee and sometimes even a glass of the illicit brew was enough to cause them to destroy property on the street.

They were a group of men who were constantly exploited and continue to receive promises from these politicians of access to flowing water, proper infrastructure and title deeds to pieces of land which were almost exclusively owned by the politicians due to impunity and corruption. It was a sad state of affairs because all they received were just empty promises.

When the time came for the first batch of social workers to undertake their placements, I made arrangements for them to carry out their field work in Mathare Valley and sent them on their first tour of the area. I thought that they would have a similar reaction to mine when they saw the state of the people there. I assumed that after seeing the harsh conditions the people in the slum were facing, that their initial reaction would be to want to make a difference and improve their lives. But I could not have been more wrong.

Immediately after the visit, they met with the department head and expressed their irritation and annoyance at being expected to earn their degree by working in a filthy slum. Around that time, most students viewed social work as a white-collar occupation, where one became a bridge between needy people and donors or social welfare providers. They thought social work was about giving handouts and other forms of aid from the comfort of an office. Some students were so disappointed that they began to drop out of the course entirely and change to other departments.

Mr. Mbithi, the department head, was not at all amused. I was summoned at once to his office where I was informed that my teaching methods were driving students away. I felt very discouraged and it seemed like everything I had tried to accomplish had failed.

Although I was disheartened, I was resolved in my conviction that the students needed Mathare and other slum exposure as a mandatory requirement for social work. I stubbornly decided to keep this requirement so as to retain only those students who had a genuine interest in social work and consequently upon graduation, would end up truly benefiting the less fortunate members of society.

THE WOMEN OF MATHARE VALLEY

A strong woman is not the one who doesn't cry. A strong woman is the one who cries and sheds tears for a moment, then gets up and fights again.

In 1984, I began visiting Mathare informally, to find a place where I could take the students to participate in field work. My central aim was for them to work with the women and children of the valley.

I did not have any lectures on Wednesday afternoons, so I used this time to make weekly trips to the slum to see the women. During our first few contact meetings, their suspicion and mistrust was palpable, and I would arrive at the meeting place only to find unattended and unsupervised children—their mothers nowhere to be seen.

Months later, I learned that they were cautious because they thought I was an undercover policewoman out to catch them in their illegal ways. They would send their children as spies to see if any police officers had accompanied me.

Most of the women were jail birds, stuck in a never-ending cycle from jail and back to prostitution or chang'aa brewing that was an illegal trade. One of the women had birthed all her four children in jail after being arrested several times for prostitution.

When the women finally realized that I was visiting alone, they agreed to meet with me. I initially connected with one lady who introduced me to three other women, and we would meet at her house, which was a small shanty that looked more like a dark hole. It was unbelievable that so many grown women could fit in such a tiny room. Since there was no electricity and no windows, it was like a cave inside with only tiny peepholes that let in thin rays of light.

After speaking with the women for a while, I realized that in order to fully gain the women's trust, I needed to act, talk, and dress less like a university don and instead be more like them. During my sit-downs in the small shanty, I began asking serious, engaging, thought-provoking questions. I enquired about their historical background and how they ended up living in the slum. I asked them if selling illicit brew had helped their children, and if the strain they went through serving multiple jail terms and selling their bodies for a few shillings was really worth it. I asked if alternative businesses like selling hot tea or firewood might have been less demanding, safer, and more profitable.

Some of them would be giggling and laughing as they answered my questions, most of them found it funny that some strange woman would want to know such personal details about their lives. I let them explore their options and figure their own destiny. I was in no hurry to push them, nor was I offering to think for them, which they soon realized.

As time went by, our meetings became more and more involving; the women became more comfortable with sharing their darker experiences and feelings about life in the slum. I inquired as to how they came to find themselves in the chang'aa business and they all had the same answer: They would do it in order to feed and clothe their children.

The chang'aa business was dangerous. Much of what the women earned from selling the illegal brew went into bribing crooked police officers or the local area chief each and every time they were arrested. They also paid young men in the area to act as guards and lookouts as they brewed and sold the alcohol. Not a week would go by without a handful of the women getting arrested, and thus the women never actually made any profit despite their toil.

Most women came from their villages with more than one child. Desperation would soon set in once it dawned on them that the city was a rough, merciless place with no jobs and no money for food, clothing, or shelter.

The few men with jobs and some money took advantage of the women, shamelessly demanding sex as payment for any help they offered and because things like contraceptives seemed like an unnecessary expense, many of the women ended up with several children. With their disillusioned husbands, having fallen into alcoholism or abandoned their families, it was up to the women to provide for themselves and their little ones.

I wanted to know what the women were doing to help their children to complete their education as I had observed that many of the children did not even complete primary school. I would ask them why the children dropped out of school, and most of them would tell me that their kids had taken to drinking and selling illicit brew. I would then ask them what they had done for their children to try and help them to develop themselves.

In the end, such questions made them realize that they were caught in a cycle of poverty. They would start with the intention of helping themselves or their children but would all end up getting sucked into this cycle of poverty. Little by little, the women began to acknowledge the fact that they were painfully disadvantaged by their life of crime and poverty.

They somberly admitted that not only were their children growing up to become teenage mothers and fathers but also prostitution was taking an enormous toll on their bodies. The risks were unreasonably high, and many of them had contracted HIV, leaving orphans behind. As our conversations went on, it became apparent to the women that change was necessary if they were to break free from the cycle of poverty and abuse they were currently trapped in.

I began to engage them in brainstorming sessions where I initiated discussions about starting alternative businesses and other income-generating activities. The group continued to grow bigger every Wednesday, although I would notice that sometimes one or two women would be missing in the meeting. On enquiring with their friends, I would learn that the women had been arrested because of brewing illicit alcohol or loitering in the streets. Other times I would receive sad news that a woman had died due to alcohol poisoning or some other kind of misfortune.

Death came easy in Mathare, and the people here were no strangers to it. Frequent imprisonment and illness was the order of the day and constant harassment by local police was considered normal. If anyone was arrested, the women would come together and contribute bribe money to get their friend out of jail. Sometimes this would go terribly wrong, and the bribe givers would find themselves locked up as well.

One Wednesday afternoon, as I arrived at our usual meeting place, I noticed that the women were very anxious. On further enquiry, I was informed that one of the women had been arrested the previous night after she was caught brewing and selling chang'aa.

The women had no money to bribe the officers, and all they could do was watch their friend get taken away and locked up in a cell. When I arrived, the women were preparing to go to court for the mentioning of her case. I decided that this time, I was going to accompany them so that I could understand exactly what they went through.

We proceeded to the Makadara Law Courts. When I got there, I was pleasantly surprised to find that the presiding magistrate was a student at the department I was teaching in. Having never been to a court chamber before, I began to wave and smile at her, not realizing that it was against court rules to do so. She just stared at me with a blank look and did not respond.

After the hearing, I was able to meet with her, and I explained to her why I was there. As we spoke, she said to me "Wanjiku, do not bother with these women as they come here every day, always with the same story. They pretend that they do not brew chang'aa but they do." I pleaded with the magistrate and tried to explain that if the woman was to be imprisoned her children would have nowhere to go and would be forced to become street children.

At the time, street children were a new phenomenon in the country. They were children whose parents were unable to provide for them, because they were ill, in jail, or into drugs and alcohol. These children would then take to the streets; begging for money and food in order to survive. The older kids would take on their parents' roles, which included taking care of their younger siblings.

I continued to explain the ripple effect the woman's imprisonment would have and after much pleading, the magistrate finally gave me a letter that I was to present to the wardens at the remand jail, in order to have the lady released. We had been in court since nine o'clock in the morning, and it was around three o'clock in the afternoon when we finally received the letter.

We then proceeded to Langata women's prison, where the woman was being held. Again, to my great surprise, I found that one of the officers at the station was my former student. Although she received me warmly, the procedure for discharge was something else entirely. There were so many offices that one needed to go through to secure the release of the arrested party.

We would go into offices, only to be informed the officer we needed to see had left to run an errand, and we would end up having to wait for hours before they returned. By the time we were through with the whole process, it was after eight o'clock in the night. While it had taken forever to accomplish our goal, we considered ourselves very lucky because the officer who was my student had been helping us through the process. I could only imagine how frustrating it was for those who had no assistance at all.

To this day, I can still remember how terrible the lady smelled when she finally came out of the cell and got into my car. She had been in jail for two nights, in a stuffy, overcrowded cell with a bucket for a toilet and the cold hard floor for bed.

As I dropped the women off at an agreed place near the General Post Office, I said to them in frustration "You have seen what we have gone through. Please never subject me to that again because I will not help, and if they catch you again you will not be released". The women retorted back in unison "Wanjiku, whatever crime we have been arrested for is the exact thing we will continue doing when we get back to the slum. That is all we have and all we can do to feed our children."

I realized then that what I was asking of them was easier said than done. I was fortunate because I had a job and a comfortable life. Therefore, it was difficult for me to truly understand their world and their reasons for leading the kind of life they did.

THE BIRTH OF THE MAJI MAZURI ORGANISATION

"If you don't build your dream, someone will hire you to help build theirs".
– Tony Gaskins

A few weeks after that incident, I returned to the slum to meet the women again. I arrived at our usual meeting place to find a fire raging close by, with everyone frantically running around trying to put it out.

Fires were sadly a common occurrence in the slum and were caused by someone within the neighborhood who had left a candle unattended, children that were trying to prepare a meal, or even a paraffin stove that had exploded. When a fire started in the slum, it was almost pointless to try and stop it because of the flammable material that people used to construct their dwellings like cardboard, plastic bags, thatch, and wooden sticks.

Moreover, due to the densely-packed shanties and huts, the spread of the fire would be extremely fast. In addition, the lack of proper streets rendered the place inaccessible to fire engines and the lack of piped water meant that little could be done to salvage the situation. Nevertheless, people still tried to do whatever they could.

This particular time, after the fire died down, I heard the women lamenting that some children had perished in the fire. Although they did not want me to discuss it further, they told me that the children who died had been locked in the house and left alone because they were disabled.

These children were usually locked up and tied to the bed, or other household furniture so as not to wander off when their mothers went to the market. I painfully came to learn that children with physical and mental disabilities were subjected to a lot of stigmatization as it was generally accepted by the community that these children did not have a place in society.

I enquired further about the total number of children that were disabled in Mathare, and I found out that there were close to 90 children living with disabilities. I decided to help the women by finding a place where parents could drop off the children to be looked after as they went about their errands.

When I started, I thought that all I needed to do was go to the institutions that specialized in caring for physically challenged children and have them take the children. This proved to be much more difficult. There was so much bureaucracy and a very long waiting list for children waiting to be taken into these institutions. As I waited for word from the various institutions I had applied to, I decided to start small and began to meet with the children in Mathare.

Initially, with the help of the residents, I secured an open space in Mathare where the children would be dropped off every day. I started with a paralyzed child called Esther who was five years old, but had the body of a nine-month-old baby.

When she was born, Esther's 14-year-old mother had kicked her and broken her spine in an attempt to kill her.

Before Esther was conceived, Esther's mother had been taking odd jobs, trying to make a living by doing whatever work she could find. One day, as she was cleaning the house of a Somali man, he suddenly held her down and raped her leading to Esther's conception. Abandoned by her mother, she was raised by her grandmother who had little time for her. Children like Esther were hired out by their parents to people who used them as beggars on the streets, exploiting their disability for monetary gain.

After learning about this tragic story, my concern only grew deeper. I ended up taking in two more children who were also disabled and neglected by their parents. Unfortunately, after some time, Esther was diagnosed with Tuberculosis, and I had to keep her away from the other children for a while until she recovered.

The open space where I would meet with the children was located in a chaotic part of the slum, full of drunk and shouting men. I constantly worried about the children's safety and because it became impossible to communicate with the children, I decided to change the venue and started bringing them to my house instead. All the while, I prayed that it would only be a short while before I could get them into proper institutions that could adequately cater for their needs.

The days turned into weeks and weeks to months and still I had not managed to get a single child into any of the institutions. I realized that I had to rethink my strategy and find another way to care for the little ones. I decided to look for some space in a safe, clean building, away from the chaos of Mathare.

After some searching, my father told me about a place called Kasarani where he had been doing some construction. At the time, Kasarani was a relatively new residential area that was coming up near Mathare Valley, with scattered homes and not much development. There were no roads and no piped water, but housing was cheap, and there were lots of quiet open spaces. I quickly identified a building that fit my requirements and immediately rented four rooms, which I paid for with my own money.

The children who visited the place experienced a whole new environment, completely different to what they were used to. The place was beautiful, and the floors were cemented with beautiful grey tiles. One young child amazed by the beauty of the place looked around and said, "This looks like good clean water." That is how the name "Maji Mazuri" —which means good water—came about.

This building was initially meant for children with physical challenges, but later on, it transformed into a halfway house to receive women who had just been released from prison and were transitioning to life on the outside. I would let them stay there with their children as they found a new house to settle into and start life afresh.

At the time, I had become a regular feature in the lives of the women of Mathare; they would always involve me whenever there was a crisis. One time, in particular, they called me because a woman who had just been released from prison urgently needed help. She had two young children and nowhere to go so she and her young ones took up residence in Uhuru Park, one of the city's public parks, sleeping on the grass without any roof over their heads.

Usually, when one of the women was sentenced to time in jail, their shanty would immediately be up for grabs to new tenants. Landlords would not wait even a single day before renting it out to someone else. Even if her sentence was as short as a week, they would still find themselves homeless, with someone else already living there.

Since I didn't know of any place where she could stay until she got back on her feet, I asked her to come and stay at my house. When the family of three came to stay with me, the woman would sleep all day from what I believed to be exhaustion, malnutrition, and stress. Her younger child, who was one year old, would cry all day long. The older one, about three years old, would just sit around looking lost and confused.

I spoke to the woman and offered her and her children a place to stay at the children's center where she would at least have food and a place to sleep. In exchange, she could help in taking care of the children. She agreed to my proposal and went on to become the first woman to take up residence at the children center. She began taking care of the four disabled children I had initially taken in, as well her own children.

The women who came to the center from prison were housed freely because it was only meant to be a temporary abode as they transitioned from prison back to normal life. As a way for the women to earn income, I encouraged them to start making tea and Mandazi at the center, which they would sell all over Mathare.

After some time, I began to also visit the children's center over the weekend because I had more free time. Soon, more and more parents began bringing their children as word went around Mathare Valley about the Maji Mazuri initiative.

In addition to paying for the rent, one of the biggest challenges that I faced was providing the food for the women and the children. My parents owned a farm in the village, and I would often go there to forage for food. I would get some bananas or potatoes and whatever else I found growing on the farm.

It was difficult at first because I did not have anyone supporting me but I had committed to provide for these women using whichever means I could get. Later on, however, while attending an international women's conference in Mombasa, I met a Canadian lady who was very interested when I mentioned to her the work I did for the women in Mathare. She pledged to support us with $30 every month which would go into the women's projects. With this money, the women were able to formally register a self-help group and branched out from the tea and Mandazi business into various other activities.

Some of them began selling firewood they would collect and cut up into pieces which were used to light fires for cooking. Some would fetch water from the well and sell for about 20 shillings a Jerry can while others would collect building materials left over from houses that had been demolished and sell the pieces to construction workers. Majority of the women also set up small stalls by the roadside and during lunch time would sell cooked food like githeri which was a meal prepared with beans and maize. Slowly by slowly I watched as the women's standard of living and care for their children began to improve.

INTERACTING WITH THE WOMEN AND MEN FROM THE MAASAI COMMUNITY

Back when Maji Mazuri was still in its infancy, I had started a tailoring and dressmaking shop in Ngong Area. During my undergraduate studies in the United States, I had taken tailoring and dressmaking as an elective course.

When I finally came back to Kenya, I set up shop in Ngong and employed eight people. We specialized in all kinds of garments including men's and women's clothes, as well as industrial uniforms. However, I soon found out needles, thread, and sewing machines were not my callings in life. The winds of fate were blowing in a different direction, bringing with them the Maji Mazuri dream.

As I continued to work with the women from Mathare Valley, I got the opportunity to interact a great deal with the Maasai, who were the main inhabitants of Ngong town where my shop was set up. The Maasai are a pastoral community who depend heavily on livestock for food and income. The women mainly spend their time at home while the boys herd the cattle from morning to evening. I soon came to learn that Maasai tradition subjected girls to barbaric circumcision rites as well as early marriages to elderly men.

My initial interaction with the Maasai occurred after I was invited on a tour of the community by a Canadian missionary named Gordon, who was working with the locals. On that day, he drove me to a certain village where he was teaching Bible classes. As I sat with a group of women at the meeting, I could tell that these people were not educated at all. Apart from one or two people, the great majority of the children and adults could barely communicate in English or Swahili.

From then on, I would make time from the University to visit the Maasai women, just as I had initially done with the women of Mathare Valley. As I sat with them, I learned how to make beautiful Maasai beadwork, and they grew to like me.

Gordon had previously introduced me to one Maasai woman named Maria who knew how to speak some Swahili, and she would act as an interpreter for the others. These interactions with the Maasai women helped me not only learn their strict traditions but also how strongly oppressed they were by a highly patriarchal system.

Maasai tradition dictated that a girl was ready for marriage and motherhood once she hit puberty. Before a girl could be married off, she had to undergo a painful circumcision rite that involved female genital mutilation. They were then thrust into marriage, burdened with a life of raising children and performing wifely duties to polygamous men far older than themselves.

On the other hand, some girls were sent off to stay with wealthy families and work as domestic assistants. The girls were tasked with house chores including taking care of the animals and fetching water from the river. In exchange, they were paid a small amount of money which they would then send home to their families. Some families would also assist in educating them along with their own children so as to provide as much support as they could to the family they were trying to help.

The girls clearly understood the responsibility they had to their families and thus worked hard to make the best of this opportunity. This was the life of the Maasai girl child who struggled in silence under the crushing weight of a cruel culture. Moved by what I saw and heard, I rounded up the women of the Maasai community, thinking that I could rally them together against the circumcision and early marriages. It came as a shock to me when I realized that the women were some of the strongest proponents of these aspects of their culture.

When I pressed further, I realized that the Maasai culture dictated that only circumcised women could be married off. These women feared that the uncircumcised girls would be shunned by the community because a woman without a husband was frowned upon by the rest of the community. Without education or economic empowerment, the women had no choice but to comply with the harsh demands of their culture.

I realized that it was fear and an acute lack of options that were keeping the women in bondage, and so I decided to use a different approach: I asked the women to recall their youth and how their childhoods were cut short by marriage; how, instead of going to school, they were forced into marriage and motherhood. Distant looks would cross their faces as they traveled down memory lane, and would narrate their ordeals with overwhelming bitterness. Some women would confess that their husbands would force themselves on them when they were drunk, even before they had completely healed from circumcision.

The ordeal would be so traumatic and painful that even now, in their old age, they still carried huge amounts of anger and bitterness in their hearts. Other women would say that they dreaded the setting of the sun because it meant that they would be sleeping with their elderly husbands, who had no time for romance or courtship.

In all this, I had to be very careful, ensuring that I didn't offend the male Maasai elders. Maasai men were extremely powerful, as dictated by their traditions, so much so that their word was considered the law. Thus, we had to disguise our plans through a women's water collection and microfinance project, so that the men would not become suspicious of our plans to go against their traditions. I even went as far as bringing in speakers who would talk to the women about health and microfinance. This encouraged the men to keep sending their wives to my workshops.

One Maasai woman who truly impressed me was called Maria. She always came to the meetings in full traditional Maasai attire and she was one of the handfuls of women who could speak fluent Swahili. She became my translator whenever we gathered for meetings. I realized early on, from our brief interactions, that Maria was bold and that she had leadership qualities. However, she seemed to be totally oblivious to the leadership traits that she possessed—preferring to let others lead the group discussions and pitch in ideas.

As time went by, Maria blossomed into an endless source of ideas for the women's group.

One of her successful projects includes a micro-finance activity where the women each gave a little money every other month for the roofing of their sheds and houses. The iron sheets would then be fitted with gutters that would direct rainwater to storage tanks, saving them journeys to far-off lands in search of water. The women would then conveniently fetch water which enable them to have more time to carry out various house chores.

The projects that they were undertaking made them less and less dependent on the men for survival and this was not at all pleasing to the men. The men began to feel like the women were standing out more in society and that they were losing their place as the providers of the home.

To sort out this insecurity amongst the men, I began to organize for small workshops, attended by both men and women. I would then invite different speakers including health workers and nutritionists to talk about the importance of healthy living, safe drinking water and working together as a team to support each other. My aim was to let them know that I am not imposing on them but trying to create a sense of community.

One thing that the women all agreed on was if they had to live their lives over again, they would have done everything in their power to escape the experience of circumcision and early marriage. At that point,

I told them that even though they could not turn back the clock, they could still do right by their daughters by saving them from the same fate.

At this, the women's minds and eyes were opened, and they began to see things differently with a new hope. They formed support groups with other women and began to come up with a plan on how to save the girls. One by one they began hiding the pubescent girls who were earmarked for circumcision. Some of them would be brought to my own home so as to save them from the circumciser's blade. Together with the women I would then make arrangements for their education and induction into more reasonable living conditions. Slowly by slowly we began to notice a sudden change in the girl's self-esteem. This was indeed a great milestone for Maji Mazuri.

THE MAJI MAZURI YOUTH GROUP

"Tell me and I might forget. Teach me and I may learn. Involve me and I will remember."

As an ever-increasing number of people became aware of the work of the Maji Mazuri Women's Initiative as well as the children's center, many of the orphaned children in the slum and those whose parents had been imprisoned found their way to the center. Initially, they would come for the free meals, but over time, they began living there.

When I started the children's center, I had envisioned a place that would be dedicated to the care of disabled children only. However, I was now faced with a challenge as the majority of the children who lived at the center were able-bodied and without any kind of disability.

As I spoke to the children, I realized that most of them were street children who did not have any guardians or role models because their parents were either dead or in jail. I took this as an opportunity to offer them some much-needed guidance and counseling. I did this by organizing monthly workshops which the children would attend. I had several speakers engage with them about different aspects of life, including adolescence and education.

I began to wonder if the families that were separated by prison sentences ever reunited after the women were released from jail. The women that passed through the halfway house all had the same story. Tearfully, they would tell me that before they left for prison, they would have all their children living with them, but after serving out their sentences, they would return home to find only one or two children still living in the neighborhood. The other children would move to the streets, where they would beg or steal in order to survive.

Tracking them down was almost impossible, and many women had given up on the search for their children. I rallied the women of Maji Mazuri, and together, we searched for the missing children, who I then invited to the workshops.

The first meetings I had with the children were held at the YMCA, which was convenient as it was situated just across the road from the university where I worked. The workshops were to be held every last weekend of the month. The main reason I arranged for the workshops was to understand why the kids went into the streets and what they went through while living there.

In addition to requesting the YMCA to allow us to use their facilities, I also asked them to provide a lifeguard who would help to take care of the children as they used the swimming pool. I knew that I needed to give the children some kind of incentive to come to the meetings and the swimming pool was just the thing I needed to entice them.

The YMCA officials were hesitant to let us use their grounds because, in their minds, having noisy street children on their grounds would reflect poorly on their image. They were also fearful that we would be a distraction to the other activities and meetings going on within the compound. I pleaded with them for the children's sake. I explained to them that turning us away would gravely affect the children's future. Without any guidance and counseling, they would continue living recklessly on the streets and eventually end up in jail or worse.

After much convincing, the YMCA Director not only agreed to let the kids in but also provided lifeguards to watch the children as they swam. Tears filled my eyes as I watched these dejected children playing in the water, wide smiles on their faces as they forgot about their woes for the weekend.

Although the YMCA provided us with a venue for our meetings, they offered no more support in terms of food or sleeping quarters. Since the workshops were intended to last for an entire weekend, I knew I had to find a way to feed the children. This turned out to be quite a challenge because the food at the YMCA canteen turned out to be very expensive.

I approached the YMCA administration once again and asked for permission to bring in my own food. This request was granted, and I immediately rounded up some teenagers from Mathare Valley who helped me with the cooking. The food preparation was done at my house after which we carried it to the YMCA in my pick-up truck. The swimming and free meals ensured that the kids looked forward to the workshops and consequently, more of them joined us in the months that followed.

Since the YMCA did not allow us to spend the night within their compound, the children had to sleep on the streets and make their way back to the grounds the following morning. This was extremely disruptive as some of the kids would get in trouble during the night and end up not turning up for the second day of the workshop.

My pleas to the YMCA administration to have the kids spend the nights fell on deaf ears. Having hit a dead end in my discussions with the YMCA, I began to search for an alternative location to host the monthly workshops.

After weeks of searching for the ideal place to hold our meetings, I stumbled on the Roland Camp, which was owned by the Kenya Scouts Association. The officials here were much nicer than the YMCA, and they showed genuine interest in helping us in any way they could. They agreed to let us use their grounds for as long as we wanted.

To my joy, they granted us full access as well as tents which the children would spend the night in. Basically, they had almost fully sponsored our stay at the camp for our first workshop. They, however, informed me that for future workshops, they would have to charge a fee for every child who attended.

The scout facility was surrounded by a forest which was filled with different kinds of wildlife. The facility was also equipped with a nice playing field and a big swimming pool. This presented an added incentive because the children got the chance to go hiking, to climb trees, and have fun while swimming in a safe environment. It is here at Roland Camp where we had our first successful workshop.

More kids began showing up and soon the group grew from just eighteen to about forty-five children. During the workshops, the older kids would divide cooking and cleaning responsibilities among themselves; they ensured that everything ran seamlessly. The younger children were also happy to contribute in whichever way they could.

When I began the workshops, I made it clear to the kids that my intention was not to judge them or bombard them with questions about what they got up to while they were out there on the streets. Instead, I ensured that they had lots of fun activities, games and group sessions where they introduced themselves to one another and made friends. I made sure that they knew I genuinely cared for them.

Once I had earned their trust, I began to engage the children in more serious discussions about their experiences on the streets. My heart sunk as girls as young as 12 opened up about being introduced to prostitution and having affairs with much older men. The boys, too, had their fair share of troubles as they mostly found themselves in gangs, trapped in a life of crime and drugs that they were unable to escape from.

After I had a better idea of the challenges that the children were facing, I approached professional counselors who could address these particular issues and invited them to our workshops. The counseling sessions involved inspiring talks, as well as real life accounts from various speakers who were slum dwellers and survivors of jail, prostitution, and street life. Most of the young teens needed reasons to leave the streets and abandon delinquent behavior and I knew they would be more encouraged to listen to stories from people that had previously lived on the street.

Many well-wishers and professionals also offered me their support either by offering their skills or by offering financial assistance. We would have sessions where the kids would sit and talk with their benefactors and some of the older kids managed to get employment in this way.

These workshops provided the reasons and more importantly answers for their problems. I realized that some of the kids at the workshops were runaways whose parents were alive and well. Like the orphans, these runaways were into drugs, petty theft, and pickpocketing.

They were nearly all school dropouts, having fallen out with their parents, who could hardly afford their upkeep or tolerate their errant behavior at home.

Grasping the opportunity in this situation, I decided to get the women of Maji Mazuri involved in the workshops as well as to help track down these parents and reunite them with their children. So as to fully appreciate what the kids were going through at home, I would ask them to create plays about their experiences. The plays were usually similar in context and were planned as follows:

Early evening on a normal weekday when most people are supposed to be having supper or preparing for bedtime, a woman enters the house unannounced to find four hungry kids looking bored and drowsy. The setting is a little room with a rickety old bed, an old mattress, and no other furniture in the room. A drunken man follows the woman, staggering into the tiny shack and sits on the bed. He looks down at the famished children without really seeing them. Their mother looks at the kids and orders them to hide under the bed. They obey. Soon, there are loud noises of lovemaking on the rickety bed. The noise ends as quickly as it started and the man dashes out of the hut. The mother calls the children out and hands one of them a fifty shilling note to buy something that might constitute an evening meal.

These plays were staged before the scores of women who started the micro-enterprise as well as other members of the Mathare community. I would have the women watch themselves as depicted by their own children and gawk at the absurdity of their reckless lives. The drama was powerful and life-changing.

The women were shocked to see how they subjected their children to abuse and exposed them to danger. In the plays, some mothers would order their children out on the streets to beg for money and beat them up whenever they came home empty handed. Others would encourage their daughters, who were as young as 12, to go out on the streets and give away their innocence to men old enough to be their grandfathers in exchange for a few shillings.

When they watched these plays, the women gasped in horror and bowed their heads in shame. Others could not hold back their tears, and they wept in silence as the message rang loud and clear. As the adults began to grasp just how much they had damaged their children, they also began to address their own issues. I began coaching them in developmental psychology and explained to them that children learn from observation and grow up to imitate what they have been observing at home. Thus, the cycle of poverty was perpetuated in this way.

Little by little, the plays began impacting on the behavior of the community. They were now a regular feature in the workshops and the whole community looked forward to watching them. The children were very creative, and the presentations would be extremely humorous, but we would watch with tears in our eyes because we knew that they were based on real-life situations. The children would also enjoy themselves immensely as they got into character and every month the plays would be bigger, better, and more interesting.

Then something amazing started happening. During the rest of the month after the workshop, some of the troubled teens started going back home to rejoin their families. As the women of Maji Mazuri began to disentangle themselves from the vicious web of chang'aa brewing and prostitution, their children also learned that they had options and didn't have to follow in their parents' footsteps.

Some of the older teens joined their mothers in the youth group while the younger children enrolled back to school with the support of well-wishers. To me, this was a sign that Maji Mazuri was finally making a positive difference within the community and I couldn't have been happier.

EDUCATING THE YOUTH OF MATHARE VALLEY

"Education is our passport to the future, for tomorrow belongs to the people who prepare for it today". – Malcolm X

The school was foremost on my mind, so I converted my tailoring shop into a learning center for young girls. Initially, when I began the learning center, it was known as a head start and was meant for the disadvantaged youth of Mathare Valley. It was common to find children as old as 14 who only had three to four years of schooling if any. This was because they came from poor backgrounds and therefore could not afford tuition fees.

Girls would often get pregnant and drop out of school for long periods. This meant that the children were always in and out of school, causing them to be left behind by their peers. Ultimately, they would give up on education and turn to business or other illegal activity to get by.

I became greatly distressed when I learned that the students were missing school for reasons that could be avoided. I pondered on how to help the youth and came up with a project which I codenamed '*Head*

Start'. Thus, I decided to eventually close down my tailoring shop in Ngong to pave the way for a learning center.

From money I had saved up, I built three classes for standard one, two, and three. I could not educate them beyond that due to my constrained budget. The school was a success from the start, with many youth from Mathare attending classes regularly.

For those who were too old to attend primary school and high school, I set up a tailoring training center at the Maji Mazuri Center in Kasarani where they could learn a skill. The girls worked hard and at the end of their courses, they would often come together and start a business in town.

Although the classes were a great help to the youth, I still wasn't satisfied with the three classes. I really wanted to provide them with a high-quality education that could positively impact their standard of living. Soon, the little learning center was bursting at the seams with huge student numbers.

I decided to move the school from Matasia, to its current location in Kiserian. The new premises were more spacious, allowing me to expand the school into a boarding facility. However, due to our budget constraints, the accommodation section was anything but nice, with the boarders having to sleep on the floor or anywhere that they could find space.

During this time, I tried to approach the Rotary Clubs of Kenya about providing some of the disabled students from Mathare with wheelchairs and crutches. It took almost a year to get some wheelchair donations from the clubs, which was very frustrating for the students. With the Rotary Club back then, it seemed that you had to have someone on the inside that could rally the other members to your cause. Otherwise, your request would fall on deaf ears.

By some stroke of luck, during a trip to the United States, I was invited to several Rotary Club meetings, where I made my appeal for funds and donations for the poor and disabled children at the Head Start Center. My cause seemed to pique the interest of the president of the Rotary Club Society, a man named Hack. To my surprise and great joy, he took it upon himself to rally the different Rotary Clubs to my cause. Soon, he had come up with a plan, not just to help the children with donations, but also to help turn the center into a fully-fledged school with proper classrooms and boarding facilities.

A few American Rotary members flew down to Kenya to see the school and the kids. Once they were satisfied that the project was indeed viable, they chose the Rotary Club of Muthaiga to oversee the project from start to finish. I almost leaped with joy as the construction began.

Today, the academic institution has grown to include both a primary school section as well as a secondary school section. They are located in the middle of a valley, right next to the highway which slopes gently towards Kiserian and climbs back up towards the city through the lush vegetation of Ngong forest. The secondary school is known as Upper Matasia Secondary School—the only Maji Mazuri franchise that does not bear the organization's name.

It is a fine school. A stroll within its walls reveals a compound that is neat and kempt with carefully mowed lawns and a network of pavements. It is a model school with an imposing storied building that houses the classrooms and the boy's dormitory.

The students happily stroll around in their free time looking rather stylish in their uniforms. It would be hard for anyone to guess that many of them are orphans and off springs from the Mathare Valley. The girls' dormitory lies in the upper part of the compound. A short distance away is a fence that separates the secondary school from the primary school.

Both school complexes are nationally recognized and offer a competitive academic curriculum to all their students. Currently, the primary school has 350 students with a majority being girls. The secondary school has 120 students.

Some of the students who are orphans, sadly experience personal challenges which we would notice during the course of their academic years. Most of them would start out doing very well in school and towards the final years, their grades would drop after every term. I then realized that most of them began to have fear of leaving the school since they were not sure they would receive the kind of treatment they were getting in the school. Three full meals in a day was definitely a privilege. We then decided to work on getting individuals who have experienced and gone through similar challenges to act as mentors to the students and show them that the world has much to offer if only they assert themselves.

Today we boast of several success stories from children who have gone on to graduate from university and get employment. Many are now, married with children and working hard to raise their own families. When I look at how far they have come and all the struggles we went through to get to where they are, I am even more convinced that I had made the best decision to return back home from the US. Even though the journey was not easy, I would never have changed it for anything else.

1. Mathare Valley   2. The Maji Mazuri Building   3. The Children of Maji Mazuri"
4. Esther, the 1st child brought to Maji Mazuri   5. The Youth of Maji Mazuri   6. The Maji Mazuri Youth Group

1. Wanjiku with the Maasai Women 2. Wanjiku with the Maasai Women 3. The Women of Maji Mazuri
4. The Women of Maji Mazuri 5. The Youth of Maji Mazuri 6. The Youth of Maji Mazuri

BITS AND PIECES OF MY TRAVELS AROUND THE WORLD

"We travel not to escape life but for life not to escape us". – Anonymous

When I came back home from the United States after completing my Master's degree, the first country I had the privilege of visiting was Canada. In 1985, I traveled to Mombasa to give a speech at the International Women's Conference about my work at Maji Mazuri. A group of Canadian social workers at the meeting heard me speak and became interested in partnering with Maji Mazuri. We worked together for about three years before they invited me to Canada to rally different groups to support the Maji Mazuri, which was in its infancy at the time.

I jetted into Canada in the summer of 1987. Rosalind, a woman I had become friends with in the years I had worked with the Canadians, picked me up from the airport and drove me to her house. She lived with her husband in a cottage that overlooked a beautiful lake on their incredibly large tract of land. Due to the long summer days, the people there could work and be productive for up to fifteen hours a day. I remember Rosalind and her husband had converted part of their land into a farm. Her husband, who worked as a lawyer, would come home after work, change into his overalls and drive their tractor out into the farm to plow the land.

I was shocked to learn that even Canada, a country endowed with abundant resources and a small population, still struggled with rising levels of poverty and an ever-increasing population of homeless people. While there, I was introduced to an African-American woman who had established a homeless shelter. Due to her work, the poor and the homeless could get hot meals, medical care, rehabilitation and work placements at no cost at all.

Today, I have become a globetrotter, traveling far and wide due to the great demands of my work. However, in all my travels, nothing has enriched my love and appreciation for my beautiful motherland as traveling to other African countries.

I have visited countries whose cities and business districts resemble small rural towns in Kenya. On such occasions, I realized just how much my country has developed over the years, and how high the quality and level of education in Kenya truly is. The skills that Kenya exports to our neighboring countries are of very high quality because most Kenyans have access to education.

Another thing that has made me appreciate being a Kenyan is our entrepreneurial spirit. Kenyans have in them a drive and a passion for developing themselves and their communities, be it through farming or other forms of income generating activities. Kenya is also endowed with a substantial transport and communications infrastructure.

In many African countries, I have found that villages and towns are often interconnected with poorly maintained or non-existent roads, with many people cut off from the rest of the continent due to the lack of any means of communication. Schools and hospitals are also few and far between.

Language barriers have also been substantially broken down in Kenya, with most people having been to school and therefore able to communicate in English and Swahili. Today, Swahili has been firmly established as one of Kenya's official languages. This is no small feat for a country as culturally diverse as Kenya, whose population consists of over forty different tribes.

In other countries, like Ethiopia, I have found that the society, though somewhat developed, is not receptive to tourists and other outsiders. I have been to restaurants where the waiters completely ignored me and refused to serve me. These restaurants, though very high end, would offer their foreign guests an appalling service. I noticed that such treatment would usually go hand in hand with a very high level of ignorance and lack of education among the population.

After visiting several war-torn countries like South Sudan and seeing firsthand the effects and aftermath of war on society, I feel privileged to belong to a country that has never experienced civil war. People in Kenya still live in houses built a long time ago by their ancestors in the 50s and 60s, unlike in countries like Rwanda and Uganda, where civil wars have shaken the population, displacing almost everyone in these countries.

War interrupts development and countries like Somalia and Sudan that have come to the end of bloody internal conflicts will now have to begin from scratch, rebuilding what they have lost in order to go further. Countries that have never experienced war are able to retain their traditions and cultures, although this can often be a double-edged sword. Some traditions can enhance backwardness by shunning developments, like technologies that people perceive as threats to their way of life.

When I think about some of the best and worst countries that I have been to, I must say that developed countries are excellent with regard to infrastructure, transport, and communication. Everything is meticulously organized, so much so that a first-time visitor can actually leave the airport and go wherever they need to go without having to ask for directions. This is a huge achievement considering how massive and complex their transport systems actually are. Aside from street signs and labels, they also have advanced satellite navigation systems, which makes traveling easy.

However, these first-world countries also have their own shortcomings, especially from a visitor's standpoint. You can feel very lonely and left out because everyone focuses on their lives and minds their own business. People there rarely talk to strangers, and so outsiders can easily feel isolated.

Life in Asian countries is very different from the organized West. In places like Pakistan and India, the roads and streets are extremely chaotic. Driving in such countries is an experience like no other. Here, both sides of the economic divide are well represented, from extreme poverty to extreme wealth.

The streets are exceptionally crowded, and I remember being constantly nervous and uneasy when walking in the streets because I would see people staring and talking about me. The language barrier also made it very difficult to communicate with people and therefore it was a nightmare of a task to do something as simple as asking for directions.

Due to the widespread poverty in these Asian towns and the lack of economic growth in sectors like tourism, it was very difficult to find a clean hotel to spend the night in. However, I found the people in Asian countries generally friendly and social, even though they had not been exposed to the outside world.

Some would be extremely fascinated by the color of my skin. Others, especially in Muslim countries, would be very surprised to see a lone woman walking about without a male escort while deemed to be dressed improperly according to their religion.

Though I have largely had good experiences in my travels, I have also had some negative experiences involving racism. To me, such encounters usually felt more like a portrayal of ignorance and curiosity by the people in each country I visited. In the Western world, people would sometimes assume that because I am from Africa, I must not have encountered or experienced some of the technologies they enjoy. They consequently would always try to train me on how to use these facilities properly, which would come across as disrespectful to me. It felt as if they thought that Africans still lived in some jungle.

"You can never cross the ocean unless you have the courage to lose sight of the shore."
– Christopher Columbus

In other places, where the population had not been exposed to the wider world, like the Philippines, people there rarely encountered dark skinned people and they always came closer to take a good look at me.

The most memorable African countries I visited were Rwanda and South Africa. I visited Rwanda soon after the election chaos that led to the infamous Rwandan genocide. I had not planned on traveling to

Rwanda, but a twist of fate led me to this war-torn country on a journey that would reunite me with my Canadian friends.

It all began with an email sent to me by Patricia and Dudley Baker, a Canadian couple that had become very good friends of mine. Since it was long and I was particularly tired, I only glanced over it and quickly came to the conclusion that they were planning another trip to Rwanda. I knew that they had been there twice before. I sent back a reply, wishing them well on their trip.

The next day, I received a call from the couple, asking me to read the email carefully because I had missed the whole point! Feeling a bit embarrassed, I opened my email account and this time; I read the email word for word. I was surprised to read that some nights before, Patricia had dreamt of me walking up and down a lush green hill in the heart of Rwanda, dressed in traditional African attire. Patricia and her husband were Christians and therefore they both firmly believed that this was a sign that they should invite me on their next trip to Rwanda, which they had earmarked for the following year. This time, I sent back a more elaborate response, giving my apologies and agreed to accompany them.

The following year, Patricia met me at the Jomo Kenyatta International Airport, and we flew down to Kigali together. From the city, we drove to a small town called Ichangugu, about one and a half hours' journey from the capital. We arrived at the local Anglican Church, through which we gained access to the community.

While there, I discovered first hand just how much the conflict in Rwanda had affected the population. Patricia and Dudley organized an annual seven-day workshop at the church, where they led reconciliation meetings and counseling sessions among the warring Tutsi and Hutu clans. It was during these workshops that I met a young woman who told her emotional tale of the horrors of the genocide and all the pain that the conflict had caused her.

Before civil unrest broke out, she lived a happy and peaceful life with her parents in Ichangugu. Sure, there had been tribal tensions before. Sporadic violence had always been expected during election periods. However, this time, it was markedly different. Nobody would have guessed that such violence and bloodshed would actually be possible. If someone had warned them, they might have fled and hidden.

When civil war broke out, her father disappeared without a trace, leaving his family desperately afraid and without protection. Soon, the violence spread to their village, and a gang of drunken, machete-wielding youths broke into their house. They raped her mother in broad daylight as the poor girl watched. After they were done with her mother, they had their way with her as well. The poor girl ended up with an unwanted pregnancy, while her elderly mother contracted HIV.

After this ordeal, life became unbearably hard. Her father was nowhere to be found, her mother was dying of AIDS, and she had a child to take care of. With her back against the wall, she decided to leave home for the city, taking her mother and child along to try and make a new life.

Unfortunately, after days of sleepless nights on the streets and an empty stomach, she was eventually introduced to the age-old profession of prostitution, trading her body for monetary gain. Years later, she learned that a man in prison had confessed to killing her father and burying his body in a nearby forest; she traveled from Kigali to her hometown to give her father a proper burial. It was during this trip that I crossed paths with her and invited her to the workshop.

This was just one of the countless horrifying and heart-wrenching stories that we heard during the time that we were in Rwanda. My training as a psychologist and family marital therapist came in handy as I was able to offer the much-needed counseling and therapy to the people who attended the workshop.

From then on, I always went with Patricia and Dudley on their annual trips to Rwanda. Slowly, families were reconciled, old rivalries were laid to rest, and neighbors forgave one another. By working closely with the local church, we were also able to introduce microfinance activities to the people of Ichangugu.

My South African experience was totally different. The first time I set foot in South Africa was in 1994, three months before Nelson Mandela became president. I had been taken on as a consultant by the Christian Learning Material Center, which was a Christian literature organization based in Nairobi. They had an ongoing project whose main aim was to look into illustrations and pictures in Christian books, specifically in Bible stories.

Back then, all illustrations in books were of white people, and there was a growing concern that Christianity—especially in Africa— was being portrayed as a religion exclusively for whites. I was assigned the task of finding out, through research, how these illustrations were perceived by black people in South Africa, where racial segregation was a big issue at the time. I was also assigned the task of finding out how such illustrations in children's books affected the self-image of black children. Interestingly, the South African, who was to be my host as well as my colleague in the research, was white.

I traveled to South Africa in the company of Millicent, an African American girl who had come to study at the University of Nairobi as an exchange student. She had always wanted to visit South Africa, and when she heard that I was heading there, she asked if it would be okay for her to travel with me so she could see the country. She also requested if the couple that was housing me could house her as well for the short period that she would be there.

Initially, she had intended to stay for only a couple of days, but after six weeks when I was ready to leave, she had fallen in love with South Africa and decided to stay on longer. Our hosts, John, and Miriam, were a lovely white couple who had a very strong Christian background, and they were happy to have both of us stay with them until my study was complete.

When I met them, I immediately noticed that they were very different from other white settlers in South Africa, in that they genuinely reached out to the black community at a time when tension was high between the white and black communities. Apartheid was the law at that time with the white supremacists unwilling to relent in their quest to rule and oppress the blacks.

Like many white settlers at the time, my hosts planned to leave the country as soon as Mandela became president. The settlers feared the black president's retaliation after they had imprisoned him for twenty-seven years for his stance against the oppression of civil rights and freedoms of the blacks.

It was evident that they were very anxious and unsure about their future. John had lived in South Africa all his life, having been born and raised there by his parents. His wife was an English woman who had moved all the way from her country to live in South Africa with her husband. John's father had also been born and raised there by his father before him. The family owned several gold mines and were well established in the land. John had known no other home. It was obvious that the mere thought of leaving South Africa was causing him a lot of grief.

The reality was that many settlers longed to live together with the native Africans in peace and harmony. For most white people, this was the only home they had ever known. Many of them were more than willing to stay and share the country's resources with the black community. Being a staunch Christian and one of the proponents of equality among the races, John would often go into black neighborhoods to meet with the people and to preach the word of God. He did this so as to bridge the gap between the two communities.

There were also some black people who felt that whites and blacks could coexist peacefully. It was these people who would introduce John and Miriam to their churches and other meetings. One native South African who was particularly important in bridging the divide was called Israel. In years gone by, Israel's father had been an employee in the home of John's family, and as a result, Israel and John struck up a friendship as young boys, which lasted through the years.

It was interesting to observe the way my white host and the black people acted upon meeting each other. Though the blacks received my host warmly, there was still an air of anxiety and timidity among them. John, however, would humble himself and show them that he was there as a brother in their shared faith. In all the meetings John attended, he was very excited to be there among the black people.

He was also very happy to introduce me and my exchange student friend to the black church members. Millicent had a very small frame, but she was a very good singer, and she would sing beautifully in every church we visited. Her beautiful voice was enough to make our host family want to take her with us wherever we went.

During my stay in South Africa, I visited a lot of bookstores in order to look at the content of different Christian books that we intended to use for our research. We also interviewed a lot of people and sought their opinions on the images in the books. As was expected, white people saw little wrong with all white illustrations in these books, and many didn't even realize the inequality represented in such books.

Black people, on the other hand, thought that all white illustrations had a psychological implication on them and their children. This is because all the images of Jesus and the angels were portrayed as white, while the devil was black. The feeling among the black people was that if there was a positive story to be told, it was always depicted by illustrations of white people, while negative stories were always depicted by black characters. This perpetuated the lie that black-skinned people were bad and inferior to white skinned people, especially in the minds of little children. It also made black people shun Christianity, labeling it as the oppressive white man's religion.

As I went about my work, I visited the slums of Alexandria and Soweto, where black South Africans lived in deplorable conditions. At that time, the country was abuzz with excitement about their impending freedom from oppression.

As the settlers prepared to hand over the reins of government and power to the new black president, the natives were under some kind of crazy euphoria which made them feel untouchable. Factory workers would not turn up for work because they thought that when Mandela became president, they would now be in control of the factories and mines. They believed the white people would now be their employees or leave the country.

I learned that white South Africans had already started selling off their possessions in preparation to leave the country. I remember John had already packed his belongings and was prepared to leave at a moment's notice, together with his wife.

Seeing the mindset of black South Africans at the time reminded me of my country, Kenya, and how we had been overcome by the same kind of crazy euphoria on the eve of our independence. Just like the South Africans, we had thought that the change in leadership would precede changes in the lives of each and every Kenyan as well.

I remember us roaming the streets as children and saying that soon we would have freedom, and even our parents would no longer have the power to order us around anymore. We would no longer walk barefoot or work in the white man's tea and coffee farms, and we would begin to live in big beautiful houses like the white people did.

We all expected that it would be a complete and immediate transformation of life as we knew it. The adults expected to land good jobs in the city and earn enough money to buy cars, land, and anything else they desired. We truly believed that life would be ours for the taking.

The reality, as we soon found out, was not as black and white as we had anticipated. When we finally gained our independence, villagers trooped to the city in large numbers in search of jobs which they were barely skilled for. This led to soaring levels of unemployment and the rise of slums like Mathare.

I told the South Africans that taking over a country was not just a matter of assuming power, but it had to do with acquiring the skills and knowledge that would empower the people to actually run the day to day affairs of the state, factories and corporations. Sadly, my words though based on experience fell on deaf ears. The people brushed me off, saying that I had no idea what I was talking about. They were behaving exactly like we Kenyans did at the time of our own independence.

I have traveled back to South Africa many times after this first visit and what I have observed is a deteriorating situation that seems much worse every time I visit, especially for the black people. This is partly because, after independence, affirmative action was adopted, and Africans began to be included in the government as well as other positions.

As these opportunities arose, however, the native South Africans found out they were ill-equipped to fill these positions, as they were neither educated nor skilled enough to take over from the whites. As a result of this, positions reserved for black South Africans were filled by skilled and learned Africans from other countries as well as those South Africans who had fled during the apartheid regime and were now returning home. Those who were in the villages were completely forgotten, and no efforts to improve their lives were made, which meant that they continued to wallow in poverty.

Today, the situation in South Africa is a sad state of affairs with the disillusioned native South Africans turning their anger and frustration on their African brothers. Merciless xenophobic attacks have become the order of the day because the natives feel that their opportunities for a better life are being handed to outsiders.

Unemployment continues to soar and crime rates along with it. Like many African countries, South Africa is fast turning into a country of broken dreams and disillusioned citizens whose hope was gone.

Since the Renaissance era, Africa has always been portrayed as a dark continent. Explorers who stumbled upon this beautiful continent labeled its people primitive simply because their skin was darker and their hair tougher. This perception which suddenly spread all over the world still persists today.

I have learned to have an open mind as I travel to different destinations simply because every culture offers a different experience. Some communities I reach out to were so isolated that sometimes I may be the first dark skinned person the locals have met.

One thing I always ensure I take with me is my culture. In fact, many times, when I am invited to speak overseas, I often make my speeches dressed in full Kikuyu traditional attire. This creates curiosity and at the end of my presentation, people will often come up to me and ask questions about my dressing and my homeland.

I see myself as a Kenyan and African ambassador, marketing the beauty of our land as well as educating the world about Africa. I endeavor to leave a lasting impression that Africans are not backward and primitive people, but rather, a warm, friendly, hard working, and forward thinking people with big hearts and even bigger dreams.

1. On My Visit to Canada as a Guest Speaker on World Kindness Day.
2. At the St Paul's Church in Canada
3. I was Invited to Speak at a Fair in New Zealand On Women Empowerment
4. At a Visit to the Taj Mahal in India
5. In India
6. Wanjiku with the Late Prof Ali Mazrui

1. I was Speaking as the Chair Lady Of the Breastfeeding Association of Kenya
2. When I Met with the 2nd President of Kenya His Excellency Daniel Moi
3. Meeting in Atlanta Georgia With the Maji Mazuri Board Members
4. One of My Recent Photos
5. Meeting with the Old People at My Father's Home in Cura village

MY CHILDREN: KIRONYO AND WANDIA

"It is not what you do for your children, but what you have taught them to do for themselves that will make them successful human beings". – Ann Landers

My two children, Kironyo and Wandia, were born under completely different circumstances and conditions. My first, Kironyo, was born on a freezing day during a harsh winter blizzard back in April 1977 while I was still living in the United States. Wandia followed half a decade later, in July 1982 and even though this was one of the coldest months in Kenya, it was definitely much warmer than the California winter that Kironyo experienced.

The first few months after Kironyo's birth were difficult for me. He was born in a country that was foreign to me. In addition, I had little support save from Kironyo's father and the doctor. I had no prior child care experience and so, I had to rely on books in order to learn how to be a mother. All through my pregnancy, I had always insisted I wanted a natural childbirth. Everyone who heard this, from my doctor to my colleagues at work and school, was shocked. They all tried to convince me otherwise, with horrible stories of children born with damaged brains and other handicaps due to their mothers' refusal to have a cesarean section. With all these mixed stories, I was worried and alone, thousands of miles from home and without any real support from my mother and aunties.

After much thought and deliberation, both with myself and with my partner, I made a firm decision to go ahead with natural childbirth. My doctor, though very cautious, had no option but to support my decision.

As I neared the end of my pregnancy, I was enrolled in a labor class which helped expectant mothers prepare for childbirth. I learned about simple techniques like breathing exercises that would enable me to maintain control of my body during the ordeal.

When I went into labor, my husband rushed me to the hospital where my doctor had reserved a delivery room. I was surprised to find the walls covered with mirrors, which allowed me to see everything that was going on. It was a scary and traumatic experience, especially as I could actually watch myself giving birth.

After what seemed like an eternity, a tiny, helpless, fragile Kironyo was placed in my arms. In America at the time, there was a general disdain for natural child rearing methods.

Breastfeeding was also a major topic of debate, and as I neared the end of my pregnancy, many women advised me against it. As soon as Kironyo was delivered, all kinds of baby formula companies delivered their milk substitutes and baby food samples to my home. This food and milk were not only packaged attractively but also accompanied with impressive baby care literature.

Once again, I was torn between these two options that would obviously impact my child significantly. My doctor had informed me that baby formula was just as nutritious and wholesome as mother's milk;

some formulas were indeed highly recommended by the hospital.

In the end, I decided to put Kironyo on formula. This decision was heavily influenced by the fact that I had to go back to work soon after the birth. My husband was already working two jobs in order to provide for the family and keep our two cars running, furthermore; my student loans were piling up.

When I went back to work, I found a babysitter who lived just across the street from my workplace. This made me feel very secure as I would occasionally run across the street to check up on Kironyo. Also, since he was so close, I could see him often, as well as bond with him during my breaks from work. The sitter took care of Kironyo for about a year, after which we decided to move back to Kenya permanently.

Once my family had settled in Kenya, I had Wandia. This time, however, I was calmer and less afraid because the women from my village showered me with love and care. I felt secure in their wisdom, knowing that it was borne out of experience.

I remembered the knowledgeable team of midwives who so calmly guided my mother through the harrowing experience of childbirth, safely delivering all my mother's children without the use of pain injections or doctors. Times had changed immensely from the painful, dimly-lit back room deliveries in the middle of the night, and I knew I was in safe hands.

I insisted on a natural birth, which my doctor consented to. Wandia was born healthy and without any deformity. My heart brimmed with love as I stared down at the little bundle of joy cooing in my arms. At that moment, time seemed to stand still as I watched Wandia's chest expand and contract, her little arms and legs kicking nothing but air. I remained in the hospital for two weeks as I recuperated.

During that time, however, the burly nurses gave me a cold shoulder. They did not attend to my needs as they should have. Each time I rang the bell asking for assistance, they always took their time before they responded to my call. This went on for about a week. Fortunately, I made a friend who was one of the hospital staff and who at the time happened to be walking down the halls of the maternity ward.

I found out that we were from the same community and because she also spoke Kikuyu, we were immediately able to relate to each other. From then on, she always passed by my private room to check if I needed anything. Between my friend's visits and my family's support, staying at the hospital changed for the better, especially during my second week of recuperation.

When I finally took Wandia home, I not only found a ready meal but also all my family and friends waiting for me, eager to see the new addition to the family. Kironyo, who had now turned into a curious, energetic five-year-old boy, came out joyfully to meet his new sister. It was hilarious to see his reaction when he first laid eyes on the infant. He clearly believed that she was a doll until he touched her hand and she responded to the sensation. He backed away, scared and confused, not knowing what in the world his mother had brought home.

Another time, as I was changing Wandia's nappies, Kironyo happened to be passing by when something caught his eye. He approached me slowly with a curious look on his face. After observing for a while, he finally turned to me and asked in Kikuyu: "Mommy, did you cut off the baby's pee-pee?"

I smiled as I explained to Kironyo that girls and boys were physically different. Kironyo walked away slowly, visibly struggling to absorb this new information.

During this time, I had taken a three-month leave from work as I had now secured tenure at the University of Nairobi. My mother, as well as other women from the village, frequently visited me. They offered me all the support, advice, and love I required.

They also taught me child care techniques and showed me how to prepare special meals from milk-giving foods. Older women also came to bless and examine the baby as was done traditionally, in the absence of a doctor. Wandia was breastfed which gave her the time to bond with me.

All through their childhood, Kironyo and Wandia proved to be resilient and brave children, which made me very proud of them. One time, Wandia was given the honor of being one of the flower girls at a wedding.

As the wedding day approached, she was very excited at her special role; it was all she spoke and thought about. However, when she asked me what exactly the role of a flower girl entitled, she was sorely disappointed at hearing that all she was required to do was carry a basket of rose petals and follow the bride and groom around as they stole the show from her.

Unknown to me, Wandia devised a scheme to get herself some attention at the ceremony. On the day of the wedding, just as the minister was about to disperse the crowd, brave little Wandia ran up to the podium and announced that she had a wedding present for the just-married couple.

She then went ahead to sing two beautiful wedding songs for the bride and groom, who were both very pleased. Everyone at the wedding stood to cheer on five-year-old Wandia as she sang her heart out.

Kironyo also proved his resilience one day, when he was forced to go on an unexpected adventure. He was only four at the time and had been attending kindergarten for a while. I had just hired a new house girl, and she was shown the route to Kironyo's school so that she could begin dropping him off and picking him up.

On the very first day that the girl was supposed to pick him up, something terrible happened. There were lots of other children from Kironyo's school that were picked up by their parents and guardians. Typically, when the bus arrived, all the children ran onto the bus, followed by the adults. My house help assumed that Kironyo had also hopped onto the bus, and she quickly boarded just as it began to head off. However, as she searched for Kironyo among the neatly uniformed children, she realized that he was not on the bus at all. She had left him at the bus stop all alone.

Kironyo, being the bright little hardy rascal that he was, was not at all worried. He had traveled to and from school enough times to know the routes and the bus number like the back of his hand. He waited for another bus, which he boarded all the way to the neighborhood bus stop.

In Kenya, young children are not required to pay to ride a public service vehicle. After he had alighted, Kironyo proceeded to cross a very busy street by himself and walk the rest of the journey home.

Meanwhile, the house help had rushed back to the bus stop and to the school in a fit of panic, trying to locate the missing boy. Tearfully, she arrived back home, wondering what she would say to me later that evening. To her surprise and joy, she found a tired Kironyo at the doorstep waiting for someone to open the front door for him. Later that evening, Kironyo told me of his escapade and listened as I gave the house help a stern warning to be more careful next time. Deep inside, however, I was proud of my son for his bravery and calmness in the midst of trouble.

THE STRENGTHS AND CHARACTERISTICS OF MY CHILDREN

"The greatest gifts you can give your children are the roots of responsibility and the wings of independence." – David Waitley

When it comes to my children's character traits, Wandia has always had a go-getter attitude. She possesses leadership skills as well as a wonderful take-charge personality that enables her to change whatever she does not like about her environment. She began her school years at St. Georges' primary school, where she performed dismally in her first end of term exams.

I remember she came home sulking and ashamed of herself for her poor showing. I tried my best to comfort her, but she would hear none of it. I told her to focus on the number of people who are behind her and try her best to increase that number. For example, if she was number 56, I told her to try to make sure that the next time she was number 50. She began to apply herself to school and within a short period of time, she was one of the brightest in her class. She would visualize where she wanted to be and with razor-sharp focus, achieve her goal.

Wandia always put her best foot forward in whatever she did, be it sports or class work. She received all kinds of high praise from her teachers. After primary school, she was enrolled at Limuru Girls High School, where her brilliance continued to shine. By her second year in the school, she had already been chosen as class prefect.

One day, she called me from school out of the blue and said, "Mum, I can't stand this school, it's so dirty. The toilets are so vile. Even the faculty's facilities are just as bad as the students'!" After we had spoken, she walked right up to the principal's office and gave her a piece of her mind about the sorry state of the school compound. Then, she asked the principal to grant her the responsibility of changing the face of her beloved school. Impressed by Wandia's bold attitude, the principal immediately promoted her to the position of health prefect, putting her in charge of school cleanliness.

Wandia also cared a great deal about her peers and always went out of her way to counsel any wayward colleagues. I remember one time during a visiting day, we were seated on the grass having a meal, when Wandia noticed her school mate jumping over a fence and cutting through a flower bed. She hurriedly excused herself from our meal and ran over to the girl to counsel her against repeating the offense. Wandia would also invite me to her school as a guest speaker to talk to the youth about how they could help each other and counsel one other.

After she had completed high school, Wandia left Kenya for Ohio Western University. When she got there, she realized that the cost of her tuition and campus hostels would be too expensive. The official university policy was that freshmen had to live on the campus. However, Wandia had it in her mind that she could convince the school to grant her special permission to board off campus. Confidently, she eloquently and convincingly tabled her submissions to a panel of university officials, detailing why she should be allowed to live at a cheaper residence. She respectfully let them know that she would be a great asset to the university, and it would be their loss if they let her go. Wandia believed in herself so much that in the end, she got her way and was allowed to live off-campus.

Like me, Wandia also has a passion for activism and community service. Back at Ohio Western University, she somehow managed to get herself a job at a halfway house for homeless and battered people. She was placed in charge of supplies and ensuring that the people who came in were not only received and catered for but also always had a hot meal as well as a place to sleep. Due to her kindness and her activism, she grew very popular at the school, especially among the international students.

Wandia's activism saw her travel to Canada as a key note speaker at an International Youth Conference. The conference was attended by thousands of youth from all over the world. My heart brims with pride and joy every time I think of my daughter's successes at such a young age.

My son Kironyo, shares a lot of characteristics with his sister Wandia however, he is unique in his own way. Kironyo was very bold and fearless from a young age. When he began his schooling, I enrolled him at Rosslyn Academy, which was an all-white school apart from one or two black faculty teachers and a handful of black students.

At Rosslyn, Kironyo quickly noticed that there was a lot of inequality, with blacks holding the short end of the stick. The black faculty held lowly positions and their staff quarters were run down compared to the spacious bungalows of the white missionary staff. This inequality frustrated Kironyo to such an extent that he got into a fight with one of the white students as they fiercely argued about it. Of course, he was sent home for the offense.

When I was summoned to the school, I took my brother with me and headed straight to the principal's office with Kironyo in tow. When he was requested to tell his side of the story, Kironyo confidently went on a rant about the seclusion, harassment, and humiliation that black students underwent at the hands of white students.

He told the principal that the only reason his case was brought forward was because he dared to fight back, instead of letting the white boy beat him. My brother and I were shocked that instead of being sorry for fighting in school, Kironyo was lecturing his principal. We both braced ourselves for Kironyo's severe punishment. However, contrary to our expectation, the principal thanked Kironyo for his honesty about what was going on within his school, and Kironyo was sent back to class.

Kironyo has an entrepreneurial mindset. He is always identifying opportunities to make some money and takes full advantage of these opportunities when they present themselves. When we moved to Kenya, I wanted Kironyo to continue with the American education system, and therefore enrolled him at a school that was offering both the Kenyan and American syllabus.

Unlike most of his friends studying the Kenyan "8-4-4 system", Kironyo's holidays were long. He, therefore, used this time to design prints on T-shirts and sell them to his peers. He would also buy bulk jewelry at wholesale price town and then sell it to both his neighbors and school mates at marked up prices.

At a very early age, he developed an interest in the Stock Exchange and stock investments. He researched on the stock market and learned as much as he could about it so that he could make sound investment decisions. His first buy was Uchumi Supermarkets, and to this day, I still receive a check in his name from this old investment.

Kironyo is also a critical thinker and a man of the people. Every morning, the Rosslyn Academy school bus would pick him up along Ngong road. Instead of walking through Ngumo Estate, which was a secure, gated community, Kironyo preferred to take a short cut through Kibera slum. Unlike Mathare, I hardly knew anyone in Kibera, and this worried me because I feared that if something should happen to my son, I wouldn't know what to do or who to turn to for help. Despite my fears, Kironyo could not have been less concerned about the immediate danger he was in. To him, it was a chance to get to see as much of the world as he could and make as many friends as possible.

In addition to his free spirit, Kironyo is also kind and caring towards the less fortunate and the old. When he was studying for his undergraduate studies in the United States, he met an elderly gentleman at his church and true to Kironyo's open heart, they struck up a friendship. Initially, Kironyo had volunteered to be driving the old and disabled to and from church every Sunday.

It was through this activity, he met the old man, and they became good friends. As time flew by, the old man's health deteriorated so much that he could no longer feed himself. Kironyo would visit him constantly, feed him and take him around the block for afternoon walks. Other times, when he had some money to spare, Kironyo would go to a nearby restaurant and buy lots of food, which he would then distribute to the homeless and the needy people sitting by the roadside.

Another memory I have of his concern for minorities and the less fortunate was when he was with me at the children's center. We had just received a boy who was homeless. This boy was reportedly so problematic that the matron had not only given up on managing him but also requested me to take him to the police who she felt would be better equipped to deal with him.

The following day, while preparing to take this problematic boy into the juvenile court, Kironyo asked me, "Mum, have you taken the time to understand why this child is behaving this way? Didn't you say he was picked from the streets? If he was picked from the streets and he is about 7 years what else could he know? He has never had a proper mentor and right now you are the only person that can be a guardian to him. Will taking him to court solve the problem?"

I found it very interesting to hear him raise those kinds of questions. It was then that I began to notice that not only was he conscious about the oppression of the less fortunate but he was also determined to fight for the oppression of children that have been victimized.

Kironyo has also always been very passionate about fighting against gender discrimination. I remember one time telling him about my father's love for bringing the family together by were occasionally organizing family meetings at his house.

Sometimes, these family meetings would be to celebrate a member of the family who had returned home safely or to say farewell to another member leaving the country. My father would invite neighbors and friends. During the function, the young men would slaughter goats while the women prepared lots of food of different types.

I recall a particular time when I told Kironyo to prepare himself for such a function during a visit to his grandparents place the next weekend. He was immediately inquisitive about the nature of the get-together and the events of the day. He had observed previous functions and was questioning the point of men sitting around the trees, engaged in conversation throughout the day; while the women including my grandmother spent the day running around serving the men, washing the dishes and never getting a chance to rest. It was then that I began to notice that Kironyo was conscious about the oppression of women. He was always quick to understand certain issues and would respectfully question situations he felt he needed to speak out about.

Kironyo was always full of energy, and during the summer holiday in Kenya, I would secretly organize for him to get a job so as to keep him busy. Knowing that it was difficult for anyone to employ a child, I would make arrangements for different people to interview him and negotiate his salary depending on the amount that I wanted to pay him.

He would be given various jobs to work on and at the end of the week I would send the money to his supervisors and they in turn, would pay him as if he was a permanent staff member. I knew that he was full of energy, and if I did not find something for him to do, he would probably engage in any activity to release his energy.

Kironyo loved to engage himself in conversation with his colleagues and forever wanted to know about their lifestyle. At one point, I had secured a job for him at a packing plant where he would interact with grown-up men. He would ask them questions about how long they had worked at the factory, how much they got paid, and if the money they were paid was enough to take care of their families.

He did not mean any harm but was curious to find out if the men felt underpaid, wondering why they would want to be stuck in such a situation. Kironyo did not understand the cycle of poverty and how difficult it was for these men to get jobs. Many factories had men lining up at the gate waiting for any form of casual employment and those that were lucky enough to get jobs knew that they could easily be replaced.

Unfortunately, because the men regarded Kironyo very highly, they not only listened to him but began to question their employers while demanding for a wage increase. When the management heard of Kironyo's incitement, they fired him on the spot. Kironyo despite being very disappointed that he was fired, was content because he got to speak out and in some form, empower these men to begin to think bigger, to want more for themselves and to ask for what they deserve.

I am extremely proud of both my children. I love the fact that their belief in equality and justice is so firm that they are not shy to voice their opinions on these issues. They genuinely feel they can have a positive impact on society. I applaud them for always being ready to speak out for the voiceless and for encouraging me to finally complete writing this book.

1. With my children Kironyo and Wandia
2. Wandia
3. Kironyo
4. The children on holiday with a friend
5. With Wandia on her graduation day At the Ohio Wesleyan University.
6. With Kironyo having lunch together

1. With My Children Kironyo and Wandia   2. Wanjiku and Kironyo   3. Kironyo with his Cousin Mukuria
4. Wandia   5. Kironyo and Wandia and a Friend Playing at a Tender Age.

WANJIKU KIRONYO: HER LIFE TODAY

"Define success on your own terms, achieve it by your own rules and build a life you're proud to live." – Anne Sweeney

Today, Wanjiku is a self-made woman who has beaten the odds to become an internationally acclaimed figure. Emerging from a humble, poverty-stricken beginning back in colonial Kenya, her will and determination to excel saw her rise and succeed in academia as well as in her career, at a time when women were expected to be laid back, docile homemakers. It has now been twenty-eight years, and Wanjiku continues to manage the Maji Mazuri organization out of her home, where her office is located.

A typical day for Wanjiku starts out at 4:30 a.m., long before the sun's rays illuminate the land and thaw out the crisp, razor-sharp morning air. In the silence of the morning, she takes the time to pray and reflect on the day that is just about to begin. A brisk, invigorating walk at the crack of dawn followed by a quick shower and breakfast brace her mind and body as she prepares to face her daily tasks as the head of the large non-profit organization Maji Mazuri.

Wanjiku is deeply involved and incredibly passionate about community service. Besides Maji Mazuri, she also spearheads a program that supports elderly people in her rural hometown, Cura. While the beginnings of the Maji Mazuri organization are well documented in this book, the genesis of her work with the elderly is not.

It all started back in 2010: Wanjiku was on her way to her parents' house for Christmas when she decided to stop by an elderly woman's house. The old lady, a dear family friend who Wanjiku had known since she was a little girl, was seated in the shade of a tree outside her worn timber house that was now in desperate need of repair.

Termites had literally eaten their way through the walls of the old house, leaving spaces between the remaining planks of wood that made up the walls. Wanjiku was shocked and wondered how the old woman's family could allow her to continue living by herself and in such dire strain.

Finding her old friend in this state of poverty and loneliness really tugged at Wanjiku's heart strings. Christmas was a time when families – scattered throughout the world in the pursuit of love, careers, and education – found their way back home to be together.

Touched by her loneliness, Wanjiku invited the elderly lady to her parents' home for lunch. Wanjiku arrived to find her mother outside working in the farm while her father sat alone in their house. He was an elderly man now, and his legs had given out due to his great age.

Wanjiku left the old friends in the living room as she disappeared into the kitchen to prepare a quick meal for them. She could hear them chatting animatedly, catching up and laughing as old friends would. They would also ask each other and whether elderly folk within the neighborhood were still alive.

Some lived only 200 meters away. Wanjiku was moved as she realized that even such short distances had become geographical barriers for them due to their failing limbs and the resulting immobility.

Later on, after the old lady had left for home, Wanjiku told her father that she had noticed how much he had enjoyed the company of his friend. She asked if he would mind if she brought more elderly people from the village to his home every other month. They could enjoy each other's company, and she could provide some support for those who had no one to take care of them.

Of course, her father loved the idea. Being immobile and well-advanced in age meant that he was not able to visit his friends as often as he would have wished. Wanjiku's brilliant idea would give him an opportunity to see more of his peers.

The meetings began with a group of about twenty-eight elderly men and women—all well into their 80s. Like Wanjiku's father, many of them were not able to walk. Therefore, Wanjiku organized for them to be picked up and brought back to her parent's house.

The eldest in the group was a man named Wambu, who is 106 years old at the time of writing. Wambu was a very close to Wanjiku's father, Julius. He would always get to the house early for the meetings and personally receive all the guests. He always says this is because his good friend Julius asked him to look after his home after he had passed on.

Over the years, Wanjiku grew quite fond of the old man, and she always prepares his favorite drink: a sugar-free fruit cocktail made from sweet bananas, pawpaw, and other sweet fruits. Unknown to the other guests, Wambu would be gleefully slurping away on his fifth glass of juice by the time they arrived.

One by one, those who were still able to walk would arrive, smiling widely as they shook hands and embraced one another. Suddenly, the house would be abuzz with animated conversation about their past, and loud laughter would usually follow as they reminisced about the things that happened long ago when they were still strong, young men and women. Through these meetings, Wanjiku has learned a lot about colonial Kenya and the history of her culture.

Wanjiku always ensures that the food she prepares is as healthy as it is tasty. Brown foods like Njahi, Mukimo, and some meat are always on the menu. After a word of grace, they eat heartily to their fill. Once they have eaten, Wanjiku will have them wash the lunch down with some tea or juice and Mandazi.

Occasionally, Wanjiku will invite a speaker to talk to the group on various topics like their health, finances or their spiritual walk with God. The old people really appreciate these topics because it provides an avenue for mental stimulation and it also helps them acquire more knowledge on issues currently affecting our society.

After the speaker has finished, the group fill each other in on how their month has been. If a member is ill and did not attend the meeting, they will arrange on how to visit him or her. Finally, a hymn and a prayer mark the end of the monthly meeting. As the old people prepare to leave; Wanjiku hands each elder a package containing some food as well as some money in an envelope for their upkeep.

The time in between the monthly meetings is not idly spent. The elderly men and women listen to the local stations which have really helped disseminate information to them because many do not understand English or Swahili.

Wanjiku is always amazed at their eagerness to learn new things even in their advanced years. Today, only twelve of the original twenty-eight members remain; the others, sadly have been laid to rest, among them, Wanjiku's father.

In her work with the elderly, Wanjiku also began a program which seeks to bring the orphaned children of Maji Mazuri together with the elderly folk of Wanjiku's hometown. She goes on to explain that as people grow old, they often feel lonely and isolated. Likewise, the orphaned youth of Maji Mazuri have grown up without any parental guidance. They neither respect their elders, nor have they learned from the wisdom of elderly.

Wanjiku's quick mind saw an opportunity for these two groups of people to mutually benefit from each other. The young bring in a sense of liveliness to the meetings and take the minds of the elderly away from their monotonous village lives. They also learn how to interact with their elders while gaining valuable knowledge and wisdom from their experienced elders.

Wanjiku acknowledges that when it comes to the truth about Kenya's history, these elderly men and women are like living encyclopedias. Through her meetings with them, she has learned a lot about life in the early 1900s, long before the Kenyan British colony was established. During their meetings, they talk about untold stories about the British invasion and the systematic takeover of African land.

Painfully, they narrate stories of colonial savagery as well as oppression and torture of Africans people by the racist white masters. The monthly meetings have offered these old people a chance to share the bitterness and anger that they have carried in their hearts all their lives towards the British. As they open up and share these experiences, they are finally able to come to terms and help each other deal with their emotions.

When asked about her thoughts on her life today, Wanjiku clasps her hands and a distant look fills her eyes. It's as if she relives all the struggle, glass ceilings, red tape, and emotion that she has had to fight through to help the less fortunate and get children off the streets.

Now, with her work at Maji Mazuri having been acclaimed the world over, as well as having received several international awards for her outstanding role, Wanjiku is at a point of self-actualization. This notwithstanding, she does not even remotely consider her work finished. Rather, she uses her weight and influence to propel her cause to greater heights. There will always be someone somewhere in need, and Wanjiku aims to be there whenever the need arises.

However, even with years of experience on the job, Wanjiku acknowledges that she still struggles to discern between those genuinely in need of help and those who pretend. There are those who shamefully seek to con her organization out of hard-earned resources meant for the genuinely less fortunate.

In her great grace, Wanjiku has often found herself sympathizing with such people and many times she has offered them jobs or training so as to enable them to support their families in an honest manner.

Other people who Wanjiku has employed include volunteers who have given themselves up wholeheartedly for the cause. One such person is a lady called Janet Wambui Kabui. She joined Maji Mazuri as a volunteer and after proving herself to be truly dedicated to serving the community; she is now a director at the organization.

Daniel Wambua, another of Wanjiku's protégés joined the organization as a young boy from the slums of Mathare, in need of help after tragically losing his parents. Through the support of Wanjiku and Maji Mazuri, Daniel was able to complete his studies and today, he is one of the organization's program managers, based in Mathare.

These success stories are precisely what Wanjiku lives for. Even though her efforts may feel like a drop in the vast sea of poverty in the slums, she is neither deterred, nor does she lose sight of her hope that one day, slums shall no longer exist in Kenya. Through the constant empowerment of the young and the less fortunate, Wanjiku is sure that her goal is within reach.

In her spare time, Wanjiku likes to keep fit and healthy. She enjoys a vigorous work out at the gym, where she attends dance workout classes every Friday. She also participates in brisk walks once a week with a bunch of friends at the Sigona Golf and Country Club.

Looking back at her life, Wanjiku quips that if there was a point in time she wishes she could go back to and live all over again, it would definitely be her childhood. She fondly recalls the freedom and complete lack of responsibility she felt as a child.

In those days, the world always had something new to offer, and every breaking dawn brought with it unlimited opportunity. It was a time when the world was not only much calmer but also less dangerous. Moreover, people had a healthy respect for each other.

On being asked who she would have loved to meet most, she enthusiastically responds "Oh, my goodness, I wish I had a chance to meet Gandhi!" She goes on to explain that she has always admired his total commitment to social justice and equality. Above all, she would have loved to talk to him about his ideology. In addition, she would love to learn his source of inspiration amidst very harsh and powerful opposition which Gandhi experienced at that time as India pushed for independence.

Wanjiku feels that creating Maji Mazuri quite literally with nothing more than a dream and with her two bare hands—is definitely her greatest achievement. Through Maji Mazuri, she has been able to live out her dream of transforming the lives of the people living in some of the poorest conditions in the world. It brings her immense joy to change the fortunes of people who used to believe that life and fate had dealt them a bad hand.

WANJIKU'S ACCOLADES

Wanjiku's hard work and determination has not escaped the eyes of local as well as international communities. Countless articles have been written the world over, with Wanjiku as the centerpiece. She has also received several awards and commendations for her stand against poverty in Africa, as well as for her fight against injustice and inequality. The following are just a few of these:

An article titled 'You and Your Child' by Chuck Soder was published in March 1982 while Wanjiku was only a lecturer at the University of Nairobi, long before Maji Mazuri was conceived. The article spoke about child development and the role that parents play in the shaping of their child's self-image.

Through her extensive interaction with authors and journalists, Wanjiku recalls one particular incident in 1987 when David Werner, author of the books *Disabled Village Children* and *Where There is No Doctor*, paid her a visit. He was the main speaker at an international conference that was taking place in Nairobi and Wanjiku got the opportunity to invite David to tour Mathare and see the work Wanjiku was doing there.

It wasn't until 1993, when Wanjiku returned to the limelight, this time as the head of Maji Mazuri. An article, penned by Raphael Kahasa, delved into her role as the founder and executive director of the nonprofit organization as well as the work that she was doing with the youth in the slum of Mathare.

That same year, Canadian journalist Linda Goyette wrote an article about the chance meeting of two remarkable individuals with a passion for social work and activism. These were Wanjiku Kironyo and Ros Shephered. Their chance meeting described earlier on in this book happened in 1985 at the United Nations Women's Forum at a gathering of intellectuals and activists. The outcome of the meeting of these two great minds resulted in the formation of the Awareness Programs Society of Alberta, a body Shephered used to raise funds for the women's group that Wanjiku had formed with women from the Mathare slum.

With time, the women's group in the Mathare flourished. In addition, with Wanjiku's help, they started a local enterprise using the funds that Ros Shephered had raised as capital. As mentioned previously in this book, they sold chicken, firewood, charcoal, second-hand clothes, and vegetables. This led to the birth of the Maji Mazuri Centre, where the women organized programs included catering to disabled children, dramas for the children who attended the youth camps, and tailoring classes for young women.

Two years later, in 1995, the *New Zealand Herald* published an article titled 'Bags sold in New Zealand make a difference in Africa.' The article described Wanjiku's tireless efforts to find a market for women's bags that the members of the Maji Mazuri initiative had made. The proceeds from the sales would go into educating the youth that Maji Mazuri was sponsoring at the time. Wanjiku was quoted making a plea to the New

Zealand Trade Aid community, highlighting the fact that a single sale could educate a child for an entire academic term. Such was the difference the bags would make to the lives of the poverty-stricken people of Mathare.

A local newspaper, the *Daily Nation*, also wrote about Wanjiku and Maji Mazuri in December, 1998. In one of their magazines, known as the *Young Nation*, Wanjiku was praised for her work in keeping youth off the streets and saving them from a life of drugs, crime, and prostitution.

In 2003, Chuck Soder again wrote an engaging piece about Wanjiku's visit to the facilities of the Miami county mental retardation and development disabilities board. This was in recognition of Wanjiku's work with disabled children in the heart of Mathare slum.

Wanjiku and Maji Mazuri have also been recognized by the Rotary club of Daytona in a special article written by the club in one of their newsletters. The article, dated May, 2005 and titled 'The Maji Mazuri Center', sought to introduce Wanjiku and Maji Mazuri to the club's members, informing them of the tremendous strides that had been taken to alleviate poverty and delinquency in the heart of Mathare.

Other articles about Wanjiku and her work with Maji Mazuri include 'Bringing Women out of the Shadows' by Weekend Duty Doctors and 'Finding the Key to African Poverty Trap' by Christopher Moore in June, 1995.

With such an amazing impact on society, Wanjiku has received a myriad of awards for her exemplary work in the service of mankind including:

- A Heron Award for outstanding contribution to the community.

- A world kindness day award that she received in Canada for her outstanding work with special needs children.

- A Presidential Award from Kenya's former president, Daniel Moi, for her role in the empowerment of women and children of Maji Mazuri.

- An award from Total for her outstanding role in environmental conservation.

In self-assured ambition, Wanjiku looks to the future with even more zeal and determination, to change not just her immediate surroundings, but to make a positive difference to the world. Issues of tribalism in different African countries as well as racism in some parts of the world have always grieved her heart.

Down the line, she would like to expand the scope of her organization to focus more on these issues. Wanjiku hopes to use her vast well of experience and knowledge to educate ignorant societies and arrogant governments, which consequently would result in a more cohesive, loving, and peaceful world in her view.

TESTIMONIALS

Kironyo

My mother has always had a heart for others. As a young child, people would tell me how my mother helped them. She is a woman who shared the same opportunities others extended to her. For example: When an American family helped her travel abroad, she in turn helped others travel to the USA.

In today's time, that might not seem like a big feat, but it was a big deal if you take into account the political state of Kenya in the 1980s.

In my teenage years, I was shocked how many young children and women she impacted.

The realization that the hundred plus children and teenagers who joined us on our "summer" train trips to Mombasa lacked basic needs such as food and shelter was sobering.

My parents separated when I was an infant. In my childhood, I hoped that they would rekindle their relationship. I dreamed of walking the street holding both of their hands.

Then one day in my adolescent years while tagging along, I observed how many lives she touches: Children sleeping in street gutters, physically limited teenager shut out by society, and women grappling with prostitution. The question I wrestled with at that stage of my life as I watched her was: How could my mother help lift the heads of this ever growing community of disenfranchised people to a dignified living, and still be expected to wrestle with the expectations of a traditional wife's role?

My mother is a bright light in the Kenyan community. I realized that my mother's work was very important to our Kenyan community. So I freed my mother in my teenage years from my own adolescent expectations and embraced the idea of sharing her with others.

I am proud of my mother's contribution to society. She brought dignity to our under-served communities. Now in my adulthood, I am proud to stand alongside all the other who call her "mom", "dear sister", "true friend".

So when someone asks me half way around the world, where are you from Kironyo? I proudly reply, "I'm from Wanjiku Esther Mukuria Kironyo, my Mom"

If after reading her story you ask yourself, what is the theme of this book? I would propose this theme: You can still help others even if you have very little.

Wandia

The World's Best Mother is a book that ought to be written by its most qualified author – My mother. Metaphorically my mother is the programmer who originally coded and constantly improved the operating system of my life.

Ever since I was little my mother has been my hero and someone I've always looked up to. She always sacrificed so much not just to raise me, but to make the lives of so many better. She is the ultimate optimizer - taking on each challenge, no matter how daunting, to make a difference. She embraces life with a spirit of amour, adventure and brass balls. She is the strongest person I know, full of love and motivation, and I am incredibly blessed to have had the opportunity to have that all of my life.

As I reflect on my life, the ups the downs, highs and lows, it's impossible to forget my mother whose strength inspires me along the way. All my life, she's been like a soft sponge which absorbs my tears and squeezes out lovely bubbles of happiness and joy. Her love is the chicken soup for my soul.

Life hasn't always been fair, sometimes it has been very intense. I fell down along the way. I got wounds that couldn't be seen. But through it all, my mother never left my side. Even from a million miles away, I felt her support. Her love is the reason my tears finally dried. She gave up the most important things in her life so that I could take on the most important things in mine.

Now, as a mother myself, I realize that the job is more important than the job of any CEO in this world. CEOs run companies, mothers change lives. CEOs make good employees. Mothers make CEOs. I may never be able to be exactly like my mother, but just the thought of filling the shoes of a woman like her makes me a better person.

These words seem so trite but all I can say to my mother is, "Thank you. Thank you for the love and countless times you've been there for me, even when I did not know it. Thank you for holding me up when I could not walk, speaking for me when I could not talk and enduring every challenge so I could stand on your shoulders. Thank you for lending me your ears and letting me cry on your shoulder. Thank you for working ungodly hours to give me the best opportunities. Thank you for the sacrifices you made to serve causes much greater than yourself, for taking care of people all around you even when you did not have to and for modeling for me that I too can make a difference. Thank you for believing in me, even when I have doubted myself. Thank you for teaching me to seek the power within, stand tall, and go forth. Thank you for showing me I had control over the rollercoaster of life and that optimism is a force multiplier. Thank you for the laughter, the smiles, the lessons, and reminding me that I'll always have somebody who loves me for who I am, flaws and all. You have shown me that it is okay to make mistakes, it's okay to cry, and it's okay to be who I am. You recognized my accomplishments, big and small, and always had a way to express your pride. As you supported my independence, you watched me fall down, make mistakes, and try to handle everything on my own. You still stood by, ready to pick me up when I needed you.

A fantastic mother, a fabulous friend, all I can say is she's absolutely Fantabulous.

Patricia and Dudley Baker

We met Wanjiku in 1988 in Nairobi when friends gave us some items to deliver to 'the project'. I'm not sure if it had a name yet. From then on we watched her helping the women in Mathare Valley and grow Maji Mazuri Intl., beginning with a chicken co-operative, a bakeshop, then on to the Kasarani home for disabled children, youth groups and the building of the farm which became a farm/school as well as the schools at Upper Matasia. Wanjiku was always very concerned that people have the *opportunity and skills* to be the best they can be and that meant standing up to unfair opposition from every quarter. She faced many challenges in organizing, financing, attracting supporters, dealing with staffing problems and finding people she could go to for advice. She is one determined woman and I believe she found guidance and support from God.

Patricia and myself began to go on some Anglican Church missions to South Africa and Kenya and eventually began leading missions to Rwanda. When Pat was praying about who God wanted on the team she got Wanjiku's name and she wondered if she heard Him right, He said "ask her". So Pat sent Wanjiku and email asking if she would pray about being on the team. She replied that she thought the mission work sounded good and that she would pray for us on our mission. Pat had to write back and say "Wanjiku, read the email again. You are supposed to be part of it – not just praying for it." Wanjiku did pray about it and felt God really was asking her to join the team."

Wanjiku's contribution to the missions was invaluable. In fact we could not have gone had it not been for her. She knew the cultures which we certainly did not. She had the experience of working with large groups of women which we did not have and she had knowledge and experience in teaching, group dynamics and conflict resolution which we did not have. In fact she did most of the work and teaching and the rest of the team helped out where we could. They were an amazing nine years of, a mission a year, watching what God can do to heal people. It has been a very real privilege to know Wanjiku and we have gained a wonderful friend and learned a huge amount from her.

Mama Konde

I came to know Wanjiku in 1983 after the 1982 coup attempt in our country Kenya. It was at this time that my husband was detained for 10 years leaving me to take care of our little children as a single parent. I chose to settle in the slums of Mathare since it was the only place I could afford and this is where I was fortunate enough to meet Wanjiku. I admire Wanjiku for her unique approach to community transformation, her confidence to approach different situations and her philosophy to lead with integrity.

Griffin Ndhine

I got to know Wanjiku when I was a first year student at the University of Nairobi, science campus in August 2013. I came across a post by Wanjiku on our student's notice board requiring a research assistant, with good knowledge of computers and proper linguistic competence (English). To cut the long story short, I applied for the job and that marked the first step into the journey of the school of life.

I have been working for Wanjiku as her Mentee and student. Working with her has taught me a lot about life, dedication, persistence, hard work, humanity, dignity and creativity. My work mostly includes:

- Field work as a talent developer at Maji Mazuri head start Academy. We meet every Saturday for our rehearsals and sessions.
- Digital/office assistant
- Assistant Workshop manager (Cura youth workshop during school holidays)
- Maji Mazuri brand Talent Ambassador as a performing and published poet.

In the time I have worked with Wanjiku, I have grown past my age. My intelligence has greatly and seriously improved and my attitude towards work is 100% positive. She has taught me to wake up before everyone and work in the morning for best results.

I must confess being close to Dr. Wanjiku is one great opportunity in life. She is one kind of a person many people wish to meet in life, but

I got the chance to work under her umbrella and watch how she runs her organisation. She gave me tasks I can describe as being thrown in the very deep end and how I managed to struggle to the shallow end alone is a great lesson to me. I am the Robot I am because of Her. Long live Maji Mazuri.

Daniel Wambua

Occupation: Program coordinator Maji Mazuri Mathare

I learnt about Maji Mazuri in 2003 after I was introduced by my sister who was working as a special education teacher at the Maji Mazuri in Kasarani. I started out as a beneficiary of the organisation. I could not afford to join the high school program until my sister introduced me to the Director, Dr. Wanjiku Kironyo who took me under her wing and organised for me to be included in the sponsorship program. She has continued to be a mentor and a mother to me, who has gone out of her own comfort to care for the less privileged and the marginalized in the community, guiding me through my entire journey up to graduation. Through her leadership, Maji Mazuri has continued to give hope not only to me but to the community by engaging them in life transforming activities.

David Mwaniki: Wanjiku Kironyo

I have known Wanjiku since she was a little girl in the village growing up. I was her teacher in class one and during the time that I interacted with her, I noticed she was a very curious student who always wanted to explore, gather information and was a very inquisitive student. I remember stopping by her house on my way home to chat with her and it was during this time that I discovered something very unique about her. She was very fond of photography, perhaps it was her way of wanting to capture moments. I had a camera which was probably the only one in the village, and Wanjiku was very persistent in always asking me to take pictures of her and her surroundings.

She was a very determined student and she would often tell me that after high school she would not stop pursuing her education until she had a degree. At the time this was indeed a big dream for a young village girl. She did indeed go all the way to receiving a PhD, and with her knowledge she has continued to have a major impact not only in our village, and society but to many countries globally.

I highly salute her for the project she initiated with the old people in our village where she has helped bring together a group of people to celebrate memories and to be counseled as well as counsel one another. Wanjiku has helped bring useful information that has been empowering to us (the elderly), inviting resourceful speakers who have given us the opportunity to travel out of our community given the fact that most of us are too old to go anywhere without assistance.

Wanjiku is a woman who has made a major impact in the community and I am extremely proud of the woman she turned out to be. From watching her as a young girl, I consider is one of my own blood children and I sometimes get very emotional when sharing about her accomplishments and stories.

Nicholas

In 1991 I dropped out of school. Feeling hopeless and dejected I began loitering the streets, struggling every day to survive. One day my neighbor introduced me to the Maji Mazuri Organisation and accompanied by my father I decided to take a chance and visit the organisation as a last resort. That is when I met Wanjiku and from then on my life completely changed for the better. She was and has always continued to be a loving and caring woman, who is focused and determined to make a difference in society. Through her belief in me, she enabled me to get a 2nd chance in my education and helped me and rolled back in school. Without her determination, I would not be the man I am today. Many times I wanted to give up when I thought I could not make it but it is through her support I was able to go through my education up to university and today I have a degree in. I am now married with children, a teacher and a councilor reaching out to young people to inspire them fully half as much as Wanjiku has inspired me. She is a great role model, a fighter, a great mother and even though I live very far from her, she has always kept in touch to find out how I am doing. I will forever be grateful to Wanjiku for changing my life.

ACKNOWLEDGMENT BY CASEY MARENGE: CO-AUTHOR

"She is clothed with strength and dignity, and she laughs without fear of the future."
– Proverbs 31:25–

"*If someone offers you an opportunity and you're not sure you can do it, say yes - then learn how to do it later*". This quote by Richard Branson is exactly what was going through my mind when one of my mentors; Wanjiku, asked me to work with her and help write her book. I was terrified at the thought of failing to tell the story of this remarkable woman as it should be told. The amazing story that is her life journey and the impact that she has had to so many throughout her years.

Wanjiku made this book writing journey everything I had hoped it would be and more. Throughout countless hours and days of interviews, Skype conversations, e-mails, several WhatsApp text and voice messages, hundreds (literally) of audio recordings, months of transcribing, writing and editing, Wanjiku was always so graceful, sometimes emotional but extremely passionate as she reflected and spoke about memories from her childhood and lessons learned throughout her years.

Writing this book was insightful, emotional, exciting and most importantly empowering. To finally be at the point where I am writing the acknowledgment when all we started with months ago was a vision and an idea of an incredible story that needed to be told, is unbelievable.

I would like to thank the amazing team that helped us realize this vision. From my mother, Mrs. Lucy Marenge who was a constant support system on those "Richard Branson" days and who helped provide more details on her memories as a young girl growing up with Wanjiku in the remote Cura village.

I would like to specifically thank James Gitau and Cynthia Oyugi, the team that helped edit and proofread this book. Your hard work, long hours and support was always much appreciated. Thank you for your optimism throughout this journey and for constantly believing that we will get it done. The photographer for this project Kevin Gitonga for your patience as we went through "volumes and volumes" of pictures and listened to Wanjiku excitedly narrate the story behind each picture. The administrative team, Jessica Marenge and Brenda Warau for your patience through countless days transcribing. To Wanjiku's daughter; Wandia Chiuri who was a source of inspiration throughout this entire process and a great sounding board, providing insightful suggestions to different aspects of the book. And finally I would like to thank Wanjiku for this once in a lifetime opportunity. Thank you for believing in me. For believing that we could do it. You did it. Thank you for your patience throughout this process. For lessons learnt and moments of inspiration. You are an amazing woman and I know that your story will inspire others for generations to come.

ACKNOWLEDGMENT BY WANJIKU KIRONYO:

Throughout my journey I have been inspired and empowered by amazing people that have made such a huge impact in my life. The stories in this book have been shaped by the contribution and support of certain people that I strongly believe must be mentioned.

I firstly have to appreciate Nicholas Oiko who was the first child we rescued in Mathare valley. He has walked me through the world of people with special needs and opened my mind to the challenges faced by persons with disabilities. His achievements in life despite all his challenges have inspired my resilient attitude in life.

Another person I particularly have to thank is Teresia Wanjiku who I refer to as "Mama Konde'. She has guided me into understanding the challenges faced by the women and children of the Mathare valley.

I cannot speak about my American journey without thanking Dr. and Mrs. Kraft who literally transformed my life, giving me opportunities that changed my life's destiny.

In addition, huge thanks to Bill and Marina who took my place as a parent and gracefully took up the responsibility of mothering Wandia during her undergraduate and postgraduate studies in the United States. They were also at the forefront of initiating and supporting many projects in Maji Mazuri through providing networking opportunities with other international organizations.

Maji Mazuri has made great strides through the support of various international rotaries including the Cincinnati Rotary, Maji Mazuri

Canada, Johannesburg, Maji Mazuri UK and USA; and the Duara chapter based in the Netherlands.

I specifically thank Rosalind Shepherd who spearheaded the volunteer program and partnership in Canada which led to connecting Maji Mazuri to hundreds of volunteers and interns that have spent several months in Nairobi mentoring as well as serving the youth and families of Maji Mazuri.

Moreover, I thank Peter Koing and the entire family who helped initiate the first school in Kiserian.

I also acknowledge everyone that was involved in the fight for our country's independence because they fought tirelessly to ensure that our future generation shall be free and not suffer from the oppression that sadly our forefathers faced during colonization. To all my friends who have always encouraged and supported me in decisions that I have made throughout my journey; I am forever grateful. From those that I went to school with, to many that I have worked with; your contribution in my life has not gone unnoticed.

I acknowledge my brothers and sisters, nieces and nephews who have encouraged, supported and helped me to build my self-confidence without any criticisms. They have walked with me through the ups and downs of my family's journey and continue to constantly motivate me to chase after my dreams.

I would like to specifically thank Casey who has played a big part in writing this book. To me she has been a friend, a daughter and a great mentor. Her ambition, focus and intelligence has inspired me to push further in my life. I am extremely grateful for her determination to complete this project and for her knowledge and creativity to bring everything together. I am grateful for her patience, her insight and for helping me share my story, turning my dream and vision to write a book into reality.

Last but not least I would like to thank God for seeing me through this far. For saving and taking care of me through many areas in my life. Looking at my background as a child, my journey was one of miracles and it's only by God's grace that I have reached where I am today. None of the opportunities I have today came easy. I did not come from a family with a strong financial background, was not born with a silver spoon and had to live through several challenges, but it's by his grace that I was able to live to my full potential and give my children great opportunities and the best in life. Growing up I watched several girls lose direction and get married at a young age, I watched families break up, but I am blessed that by his grace my family stuck together through the difficulties and challenges that we went through and for that I am grateful. It is my hope that this book will be a testament to my life's journey. That it will inspire even one person to chase after his or her dreams, regardless of circumstance, believing that we have within us the strength to achieve anything that we set our mind to.

29194746R00127

Printed in Great Britain
by Amazon